TABLE OF CONTENTS

ADDISON-WESLEY'S
WEB WIZARD SERIES

THE WEB WIZARD'S GUIDE TO XHTML™

CHERYL M. HUGHES

PEARSON

Addison
Wesley

Boston San Francisco New York
London Toronto Sydney Tokyo Singapore Madrid
Mexico City Munich Paris Cape Town Hong Kong Montreal

Senior Acquisitions Editor: *Michael Hirsch*
Project Editor: *Maite Suarez-Rivas*
Senior Production Supervisor: *Juliet Silveri*
Marketing Manager: *Michelle Brown*
Composition and Art: *Gillian Hall, The Aardvark Group*
Copyeditor: *Carol Noble*
Proofreader: *Holly McLean-Aldis*
Cover and Interior Designer: *Leslie Haimes*
Text and Cover Design Supervisor: *Gina Hagen Kolenda/Joyce Cosentino Wells*
Print Buyer: *Caroline Fell*

Figures 1.9, 1.10, 1.12, 3.13 copyright © 1994–2003 W3C® (Massachusetts Institute of Technology, European Research Consortium for Informatics and Mathematics, Keio University). All Rights Reserved.

Access the latest information about Addison-Wesley titles from our World Wide Web site: *http://www.aw-bc.com/computing*

Many of the designations used by manufacturers and sellers to distinguish their products are claimed as trademarks. Where those designations appear in this book, and Addison-Wesley was aware of a trademark claim, the designations have been printed in initial caps or all caps.

The programs and applications presented in this book have been included for their instructional value. They have been tested with care, but are not guaranteed for any particular purpose. The publisher does not offer any warranties or representations, nor does it accept any liabilities with respect to the programs or applications.

Library of Congress Cataloging-in-Publication Data
Hughes, Cheryl (Cheryl Marie), 1970-
    The Web wizard's guide to xhtml / Cheryl M. Hughes.
      p. cm. -- (Addison-Wesley's Web wizard series)
    Includes bibliographical references.
    ISBN 0-321-17868-8
   1. XML (Document markup language) 2. Web sites--Design. I. Title. II. Series.

   QA76.76.H94H84 2004
   006.7'4--dc22   2004008230

For information on obtaining permission for the use of material from this work, please submit a written request to Pearson Education, Inc., Rights and Contracts Department, 75 Arlington St., Suite 300, Boston, MA 02116 or fax your request to 617-848-7047.

12345678910—QWT—060504

PREFACE

About Addison-Wesley's Web Wizard Series

The beauty of the Web is that, with a little effort, anyone can harness its power to create sophisticated Web sites. *Addison-Wesley's Web Wizard Series* helps readers master the Web by presenting a concise introduction to one important Internet topic or technology in each book. The books start from square one and assume no prior experience with the technology being covered. Mastering the Web doesn't come with a wave of a magic wand, but by studying these accessible, highly visual textbooks, readers will be well on their way.

The series is written by instructors familiar with the challenges beginners face when first learning the material. To this end, the Web Wizard books offer more than a cookbook approach: they emphasize principles and offer clear explanations, giving the reader a strong foundation of knowledge on which to build.

Numerous features highlight important points and aid in learning:

☆ Tips—important points to keep in mind

☆ Shortcuts—time-saving ideas

☆ Warnings—things to watch out for

☆ Review questions and hands-on exercises

☆ Online references—Web sites to visit for more information

Supplements

Supplementary materials for the books, including updates, additional examples, and source code are available at `http://www.aw-bc.com/webwizard`. Additional supplements for instructors adopting a book from the series include: instructors' manuals, test banks, PowerPoint slides, solutions, and Course Compass—a dynamic online course management system powered by Blackboard. Instructors should contact the local Addison-Wesley sales representative for access to these.

About This Book

This book is an introduction to using XHTML for Web site development. No previous programming experience is required. The book is a visual learning tool for students and developers. It uses dozens of code examples to illustrate different XHTML techniques.

The book also contains a wealth of end-of-chapter review material with many questions and hands-on assignments derived from actual classroom assignments and projects. Since skill levels can vary greatly, many hands-on exercises have optional portions that vary in level of difficulty. If you are reading this book without taking a class, try one or two hands-on exercises in each chapter to apply the material. Like learning to ride a bike, the best way to learn a new language is to practice.

Acknowledgments

This book is dedicated to my niece, Kylie, who just celebrated her first birthday, to Tabitha, and to the rest of my family for their constant love and support. I'd like to thank the wonderful staff at Addison-Wesley who made this book possible: Michael Hirsch, Maite Suarez-Rivas, Lesly Hershman, Juliet Silveri, the copyeditor Carol Noble, and the compositor and artist Gillian Hall. I'd also like to thank my students and colleagues at Harvard—I hope that I've been able to give back half as much as I've received from my teaching experience.

In addition, the book reviewers offered many great ideas and comments that truly made this a better book. These reviewers include:

Robin Snyder
Savannah State University

Michael Sauers
Internet Trainer, Bibliographical Center for Research

Andrew Roderick
Department of Instructional Technologies, San Francisco State University

Virginia DeBolt
Austin Community College

Peter L. Kantor
Hudson Valley Community College

Ann-Marie M. Neary
Assistant Professor of Interactive Multimedia, Delaware County Community College

Jerrold Maddox
Pennsylvania State University

Marjan Trutschl
Louisiana State University, Shreveport

Stephanie Smullen
University of Tennessee, Chattanooga

Cheryl M. Hughes
April 2004

CHAPTER ONE

XHTML AND THE WORLD WIDE WEB

The Extensible HyperText Markup Language, XHTML, is the newest of the World Wide Web's markup languages. XHTML is based on its predecessor language, HTML, which makes it compatible with current Web browsers and technologies. XHTML is also compatible with new XML-based technologies so that it will be compatible with future technologies. In this chapter you will learn about markup languages and the benefits of XHTML.

◎◎ Chapter Objectives

☆ Provide a brief introduction to how the Web works

☆ Review the history of markup languages

☆ Describe the differences and similarities between XML, HTML, and XHTML

☆ Show examples of HTML and XHTML documents, and discuss the differences between them

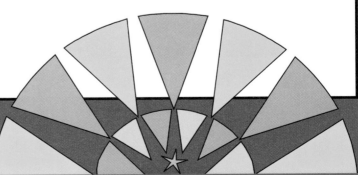

◎◎ Introduction

Welcome to the future of the World Wide Web! **Extensible HyperText Markup Language (XHTML)** is quickly becoming a cornerstone in the transition of Web technologies to the new Extensible Markup Language (XML) standards. XHTML is the successor to the HyperText Markup Language (HTML), bridging the gap between old and new technologies by being compatible with both.

◎◎ The World Wide Web and Markup Languages

Web Fundamentals

Before we delve into the details of the XHTML language, it is important to understand how the World Wide Web (the Web) works. The Web is only one of many applications that are part of the Internet. Email, newsgroups, file transfer (ftp), and telnet are a few other common Internet applications. Computers that are connected to the Internet use a suite of technologies, known as **communication protocols**, in order to transfer data. The **World Wide Web Consortium** (W3C) created these protocols as common standards so that computers built by different vendors or running different operating systems can communicate with each other (see the Tip below for information about the W3C).

The protocol that the Web uses is called **HyperText Transfer Protocol** (HTTP). Using a standard protocol like HTTP allows a computer running the Windows operating system to request and receive Web pages written in XHTML that reside on computers running the Unix operating system. Because they all use the same standard languages to communicate, it doesn't matter that they are running operating systems that would otherwise be completely incompatible.

☆**TIP**   **The World Wide Web Consortium**—`http://www.w3c.org`

The organization that is responsible for creating and maintaining Web-based protocols is the World Wide Web Consortium (W3C). The W3C developed the specifications for XHTML that you'll learn about in this book, along with many other specifications, including HTTP, HTML, CSS, URL/URI, and XML. The W3C Web site is an invaluable resource for information about current and pending technologies.

The W3C was established in 1994 by Tim Berners-Lee, one of the original founders of the World Wide Web, and is located at the Massachusetts Institute of Technology (MIT) in Cambridge, Massachusetts. The charter of the W3C, according to its Web site, is "to lead the World Wide Web to its full potential by developing common protocols that promote its evolution and ensure its interoperability." The W3C has played a major role in the promotion and growth of Internet technologies, and has helped to keep these technologies universal.

Web Browsers and Web Servers

The Web works using a **client-server model** architecture. This model is very simple: It assumes there is a computer (or computers) that has data, and that there are other computers that want this data. A good analogy of a client-server relationship would be a fast-food restaurant, like Wendy's. In this example, Wendy's would be the server because it has something to serve: burgers, fries, salads, drinks, desserts, and so on. The restaurant can be located by its address so that it can be found using the phonebook. The clients would be the customers who come to Wendy's for lunch and request the items that Wendy's has to serve. In order for the customers to get their lunch, they must first find the restaurant, travel there, order their food off of the menu, and pay the cashier. At the end of the transaction, they leave the restaurant and there is no further relationship unless they return for lunch another day.

The client-server model on the Web works in much the same way. When you surf the Web, your Web browser is a client: It makes requests to server computers that contain the Web pages you would like to view. The servers are always connected to the Internet (in order to receive requests from clients around the clock) and run a program called a **Web server** that listens for clients to make requests for Web pages that reside on the server. When you want to view a Web page, your Web browser makes a request to the server using the Uniform Resource Locator (URL), of the Web page you wish to view. HTTP, as mentioned above, is the protocol that Web clients and Web servers use to communicate with each other.

Let's look at an example. First, it's important to know the parts of a URL:

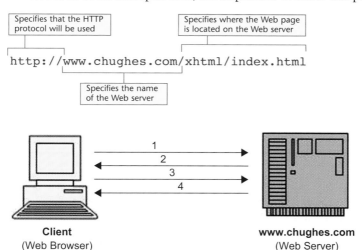

Figure 1.1 Client-Server Model for Web Servers and Web Browsers

Figure 1.1 shows how the transaction between the Web browser and Web server takes place:

1. The Web browser makes a request to the server with the name of `www.chughes.com` for the Web page called `xhtml/index.html`.

2. The server at `www.chughes.com`, which is running an HTTP server that is listening for requests, receives the request for xhtml/index.html and locates the document.

3. The server then sends back the content of the requested page to the client.

4. The browser receives the information from the server and displays the page in your browser window. The transaction is now complete.

Web servers can serve many document types, not just HTML or XHTML. Web servers can contain word processing, spreadsheet, graphical, or multimedia documents, and can serve them all via the HTTP protocol. However, the client making the request needs to know how to interpret the document being sent back. For example, if you request a spreadsheet, the server will have no problem sending that document to you via HTTP. If you do not have a program, such as Microsoft Excel, that can interpret this document type on your computer, you will not be able to view the file.

Overview of Markup Languages

A **markup language** is simply a set of rules that defines the layout, format, or structure of text within a document. After markup instructions are added to a document, the document must be read, or processed, by a program that knows how to interpret the markup elements.

Markup languages existed long before the World Wide Web. Work began in the 1960s to develop a standardized document markup language that would be platform- and program-independent. The **Standard Generalized Markup Language** (SGML) was the result of this initiative and was the first standardized markup language to gain acceptance. However, it wasn't until the Web exploded in popularity in the mid-1990s that the benefits of an open standard for markup languages became overwhelmingly apparent.

The Standard Generalized Markup Language (SGML)

SGML is the ancestor of, and provides the framework for, current Web markup languages, including XHTML, XML, and HTML. SGML was developed as a markup language for large documents, such as technical documentation. It was adopted as an international standard by the **International Organization for Standards** (ISO) in 1986, and has been widely used by many industries, including the automotive industry, the health care industry, the IRS, and the United States Department of Defense, for large-scale documentation projects. Its primary strength is providing a standard format and structure for large documents, therefore allowing these documents to be used by a number of programs. SGML provides a framework for creating other languages.

However, SGML is extremely complex, and thus very expensive. SGML has proved useful mainly to corporations and organizations that have the expertise and budget to implement the expansive SGML specification. Because of these constraints, it has not gained wide acceptance in the marketplace for small- or medium-sized projects.

HTML—The First Language of the World Wide Web

When the World Wide Web was in its infancy in the late 1980s and early 1990s, SGML was the perfect tool for building the markup language that would be used to create documents for this new medium. HTML was developed as a lightweight SGML program by researchers in the **European Organization for Nuclear Research** (CERN) in the early 1990s. CERN had been involved with working on the SGML specification for many years. HTML was much smaller than SGML and gained widespread acceptance very quickly. It provided content developers with a portable document format that was not tied to any particular program or platform, and being an open standard, it was completely free to use. HTML was adopted shortly thereafter by the W3C, which continues to maintain the HTML specification, currently at version 4.01. Figure 1.2 shows how Web markup languages have evolved from SGML.

Because HTML documents are simple text documents embedded with markup elements, they are completely portable across platforms and programs. HTML documents can be displayed using any program running on any operating system that knows how to interpret the HTML language. This gave developers an incredible amount of flexibility, and allowed them to move files freely among platforms and programs. For example, an HTML file created with a Macintosh text editor would look the same when opened in a Windows text editor, and would be displayed the same when viewed using Netscape Navigator or Internet Explorer, either on a Mac or PC.

Limitations of HTML

As Web technologies continue to advance at a very rapid pace, HTML has been pushed to its limits by developers and vendors. Ironically, the traits of HTML that helped build its popularity—its small size, limited number of elements, and ease of use—have become its downfall. HTML is a fixed specification with a finite set of elements. It's not extendable, and as a result of this limitation, Web developers and software vendors have stretched the usefulness of HTML almost to a breaking point. Browser vendors, such as Microsoft and Netscape, have added proprietary features and additional HTML elements to their browsers based on demands for more functionality, but by doing this they have compromised one of the most important benefits that HTML has to offer—portability. Given these proprietary additions to particular browsers, HTML pages developed for use in one Web browser may not display the same way when displayed in another browser or on another platform.

Even though HTML has syntax rules, Web browsers have always been fairly forgiving in that they allow poorly written HTML code to be displayed. If a browser encounters code that is written incorrectly, it can usually compensate and will display the content. This is unfortunate in that it has allowed millions of poorly written pages to be published on the Web. It is also unfortunate because the newest breed of Web clients, including cell phones, PDAs, and other devices, are not as forgiving as Web browsers and will either display the pages incorrectly or not at all.

Despite all of its benefits and the revolution it helped to spark, HTML has some serious limitations that inhibit its future usefulness as Internet technologies continue to advance:

☆ HTML elements are primarily used for defining presentation and formatting styles, but they do not provide any information about the data itself.

☆ HTML has a finite number of elements, which cannot be extended or customized.

☆ HTML does not force documents to adhere to strict syntax rules, making it difficult for parsers to interpret poorly written code.

☆ Until recently, Web browsers were the primary client program used to view content on the Web. However, HTML's limitations are further being felt with the introduction of new technologies, such as wireless devices like cell phones, voice and speech programs, and PDAs.

As a result of these limitations, the most recent version of HTML, HTML 4.01, will be the last. The first version of XHTML, 1.0, was released by the W3C in 2000 as the successor technology to HTML.

XML—The Future of Web Markup Languages

The need for a new and better language became apparent as Web developers and vendors became more painfully aware of the limitations of HTML. In addition, many companies were adding transactional functionality to their Web sites, such as allowing visitors to purchase items and services online. As opposed to the first generation of Web sites, which mainly provided static information that was easily stored as text, these new Web sites relied heavily on data gathered from different sources, such as databases, news feeds, and other Web sites. The result was XML.

The first recommendation, XML 1.0, was released in 1998. The XML family of technologies was developed to separate document data from presentation and to give developers the ability to extend the element sets of XML languages as needed. However, XML itself is not a language—it is a **meta language**, which is a set of rules used for building markup languages. Structured languages can be developed that describe certain types of data rather than just the presentation of the data. Such structured languages include elements that describe documents containing information about an account, an item, a service, or a transaction. XHTML is an application of XML that is used for formatting Web documents. There are many other XML languages, some still under development, such as MathML, an XML application used for marking up mathematical notations.

Following are a few of the benefits of XML:

☆ It allows the data to be self-describing, as opposed to being limited by a predefined set of elements.

☆ You can provide rules for XML elements that limit the type of data an element can contain, such as only letters, only numbers, or a certain number of characters.

☆ It lets you create custom data structures for industry-specific or company-specific needs.

☆ Because XML describes data, you present the data can any number of ways by applying different presentation styles.

☆ It gives you a rich set of tools for linking.

☆ You can use it to interchange data between propriety formats and between databases or data structures.

☆ You can use the tools to define a standard syntax for many markup languages.

☆ It has much more robust and reliable data searching capabilities than HTML.

Despite the hype around XML and its related technologies, not many mainstream programs support it. For example, in order to view XML documents you need a Web browser that supports it. Most current releases of Internet Explorer and Netscape Navigator have only minimal support for XML. Older browsers do not support XML at all. This compatibility issue between old and new technologies was the primary reason that XHTML was created.

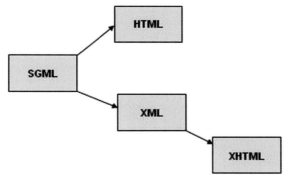

Figure 1.2 Origins of Markup Languages

◎◎ XHTML–The Merging of Past and Present

The **Extensible HyperText Markup Language** (XHTML) is the successor to HTML. The W3C released the first recommendation, XHTML 1.0, on January 26, 2000. The second edition of the recommendation was released on August 1, 2002. The recommendation states that XHTML is "a reformulation of HTML 4 in XML 1.0." Basically, XHTML gets its element set from HTML 4.01, which was released in 1997, but is written as XML This makes it compatible with current browsers, and because it is written as XML , it will also be compatible with future browsers and Web agents that require XML syntax. XHTML is truly the best of both worlds as it allows Web developers to create pages that are backward- and forward-compatible.

Following is an excerpt from the W3C Web site regarding the development of XHTML:

> *XHTML 1.0 is the first major change to HTML since HTML 4.0 was released in 1997. It brings the rigor of XML to Web pages and is the keystone in W3C's work to create standards that provide richer Web pages on an ever increasing range of browser platforms including cell phones, televisions, cars, wallet-sized wireless communicators, kiosks, and desktops.*

XHTML 1.0 reformulates HTML as an XML application. This makes it easier to process and easier to maintain. XHTML 1.0 borrows elements and attributes from W3C's earlier work on HTML 4, and can be interpreted by existing browsers, by following a few simple guidelines. This allows you to start using XHTML now!

As its name implies, XHTML is extensible, meaning that its element set is not finite, like the element set of HTML. Like any XML language, XHTML can be extended to add elements if needed or it can incorporate elements from various XML languages into its element set. Keep in mind, however, that if your goal is to keep XHTML compatible with current browsers, you may not be able to use some of its more advanced features. But if your documents are written in XHTML now, you will be able to integrate these features with ease as soon as they become mainstream. We explore some of these exciting new features later in the book.

XHTML Document Building Blocks

Like any language, XHTML has a number of building blocks that are used to create complete documents. The English language, for example, is made up of nouns, verbs, adjectives, adverbs, prepositions, and so on, which are used in conjunction with each other to form sentences and paragraphs. This section covers the building blocks of XHTML that are used to create all XHTML documents.

Both HTML and XHTML provide language building blocks that can be added to any text document. Web browsers such as Netscape Navigator or Internet Explorer know how to interpret these elements in order to present the document based on formatting rules.

Elements

XHTML elements are the core components of XHTML documents and are used to describe the data in a document. Elements are like nouns in the English language. Elements are the **markup**, or formatting instructions, of the XHTML document. Elements define the text styles, formatting, links, and other pieces of the document. The terms **element** and **tag** are sometimes used interchangeably, but strictly speaking, a tag is a piece of an element. XHTML element names must be written in lowercase letters. All elements, except for empty elements (which you will read about shortly), consist of three pieces:

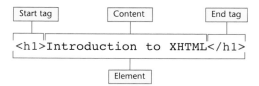

The `<h1>` and `</h1>` tags turn the heading formatting style on and off for the text Introduction to XHTML. The entire piece of code, including the opening and ending tags, and the enclosed text is known as an element.

Empty Elements

Empty elements are used primarily to describe pieces of data that don't contain any content. For example, some common empty elements in HTML are `<br>` for *line break*, `<img>` for *image*, and `<p>` for *paragraph*. In XML and XHTML, all elements must have a start tag and an end tag. The XML specification provides a shortcut for writing an empty element using a single tag. Here is how to write these empty HTML elements as empty XHTML elements:

```
<br />
<img />
<p />
```

Empty elements, unlike other elements, have only one tag. The syntax is similar to a start tag, but includes a forward slash, `/`, before the ending `>` character.

☆**WARNING** Empty Element Compatibility

We have constructed the empty elements in this section by placing a space character between the end of the element name and the closing `/>` characters. The practice of adding that extra space is not part of the syntax rules for either XML or XHTML. The primary reason for adding the space is to make this code compatible with older versions of Web browsers. Because HTML does not require end tags for these elements, most older browsers, and some of the new ones, do not know how to handle this new empty element syntax. By putting this space in the tag, we allow browsers to interpret this syntax correctly, which helps preserve the backward compatibility of XHTML.

Attributes

XHTML **attributes** are pieces of information that help to describe elements. Some elements have required attributes; others are optional and depend on the content that is being marked up. Attributes are referred to as **name-value pairs** and have the following syntax: The name of the attribute is on the left, followed by an equal sign, then the value. Let's look at a few examples:

```
1   <a href="http://chughes.com">Click here</a>
2   <img src="/images/picture.gif" id="Picture of House" />
```

The example on line 1 is the `<a>` element with one attribute. The attribute name is `href`, and the value of this attribute is `http://chughes.com`. The example on line 2 is the `<img>` element with two attributes, `src` and `id`. It is also an empty element.

Following are a few rules about XHTML attributes:

1. Attributes are always contained within the start tag of an element.

2. Names must be in lowercase letters.

3. Attributes must have a value that is surrounded by quotes.

> ☆ **TIP**   **XHTML Core Attributes**
>
> In the XHTML 1.0 specification, there are a set of core attributes that can be used with most XHTML elements. They are not valid in `<base>`, `<head>`, `<html>`, `<meta>`, `<param>`, `<script>`, `<style>`, and `<title>` elements:
>
> 1. `id`—Document-wide unique id
> 2. `class`—List of classes of the element
> 3. `style`—Associated style information
> 4. `title`—Advisory title/amplification

Comments

Comments in XHTML are notations that are ignored by programs and parsers. The syntax of an XHTML comment is identical to HTML and XML comments. You can use comments to document your code, add additional information about a piece of data, add visual breaks, or add information that other people working on or using your document would find useful. Following is an example of a comment:

```
<!-- This is a comment -->
```

Comments start with `<!--`, followed by the body of the comment, and end with `-->`. Throughout this book, we print comments in italics so that they stand out in code samples. This is not a syntax requirement. Following are some more examples of comments:

```
1   <!--Changes made by Jim on 06/23/02   -->
2   <!-- New section begins here -->
3   <!-- This document provides an introduction to XHTML -->
```

The XML Declaration

The XML declaration defines which version of XML the document is using. Stating which version of XML is being used is important in order not to confuse parsers and programs as more versions of XML are developed. This declaration always appears as the first line in an XML document. It cannot be preceded by any blank lines or whitespace. The declaration tag begins with `<?xml` and ends with `?>`. The XML declaration can contain the following three attributes: `version`, `encoding`, and `standalone`. Although the XML declaration is optional in XML and XHTML, it is good practice to at least declare the version of XML being used:

```
<?xml version="1.0"?>
```

> ☆ **WARNING**   **XML Declaration and Older Browsers**
>
> Old versions of Web browsers—Internet Explorer and Netscape Navigator 3 for example—have no built-in support for XML and will therefore not recognize the XML declaration as part of the markup. These browsers may display the text of the declaration in the browser window. If you need to make your XHTML pages compatible with very old browser versions, you can omit the XML declaration, although this practice is not recommended. Future versions of XML and XHTML may require this declaration, so adding it is a good habit to establish.

Currently, the only released version of XML is 1.0, but this will change, and declaring the version that your document is using will help parsers and programs interpret the document.

The second piece of information that the declaration can contain is the encoding attribute, which defines the character set that the document uses. A character set is a grouping of characters, such as the Latin character set, a character set of symbols, or a character set of Greek letters. This attribute is optional in the XML declaration, and if no character set is defined, the default is UTF-8, which is the 8-bit Unicode character-encoding scheme. All XML processors are required to handle UTF-8, which is why it is the default character set. Other character sets include UTF-16, UTF-32, and ISO-10646-UCS-2. There are thousands of character sets available. See the links at the end of the chapter for more information.

```
<?xml version="1.0" encoding="UTF-8"?>
```

The third piece of information that the XML declaration can contain is the standalone attribute. The value for this attribute must be either yes or no. This attribute is also optional, and the default value is no. This attribute tells the processor whether this document contains all of the pertinent information within itself or relies on external **Document Type Definitions** (DTDs) for its declarations. Setting this value to yes tells the processor that everything needed to process the document is within the document, and to ignore any references to external files. Setting the value to no tells the processor that the document can reference external files.

```
<?xml version="1.0" encoding="UTF-8" standalone="no"?>
```

The Three Flavors of XHTML 1.0

The XHTML 1.0 specification comes in three "flavors" or versions. XHTML authors can choose the version that best fits the needs of their documents by inserting a declaration line at the beginning of the document, as in the XHTML example in Figure 1.7 on line 2. This is known as the **Document Type Definition** (DOCTYPE) **declaration**. This declaration is part of the document prolog, which you'll learn about in Chapter Two.

The DTD is the specification from the W3C that defines the language, including the elements and attributes. The declaration was optional for HTML documents, but is required for XHTML documents, and it needs to match one of the DTDs for the three flavors of XHTML. The table in Figure 1.3 defines each of the three flavors and when they should be used, and shows the DOCTYPE declaration for each and where you can view the DTD on the Web.

☆**WARNING**   **XHTML Frames**

Avoid developing documents with frames if possible because frames are not supported by all current browsers, including text-based browsers and browsers used by visually impaired users. Frames are also not supported by most non-Web browsers, including browsers on cell phones and PDAs. Layouts using frames should be replaced with tables and other layouts whenever possible.

XHTML 1.0 Version Descriptions

XHTML Transitional

XHTML Transitional is currently the most-used version of XHTML 1.0. This version most closely resembles HTML 4.0.1 and is the best choice when documents need to use HTMLs presentational elements or when pages need to be developed without using style sheets. Use this version if you want to convert existing HTML pages to XHTML. The caveat to the Transitional version is that it contains support for certain elements and attributes that are being deprecated, or phased out. It also does not contain support for frames.

```
<!DOCTYPE html
       PUBLIC "-//W3C//DTD XHTML 1.0 Transitional//EN"
       "http://www.w3.org/TR/xhtml1/DTD/xhtml1-transitional.dtd">
```

On the Web: http://www.w3.org/TR/xhtml1/DTD/xhtml1-transitional.dtd

XHTML Frameset

XHTML Frameset should be used when your documents need to use the frame elements that partition the browser into multiple independent windows. The element set for this version contains all of the elements from XHTML Transitional plus the elements needed to support frames, such as `<frame>` and `<frameset>`.

```
<!DOCTYPE html
       PUBLIC "-//W3C//DTD XHTML 1.0 Frameset//EN"
       "http://www.w3.org/TR/xhtml1/DTD/xhtml1-frameset.dtd">
```

On the Web: http://www.w3.org/TR/xhtml1/DTD/xhtml1-frameset.dtd

XHTML Strict

XHTML Strict most closely represents the future of XHTML. The element set for XHTML Strict contains a subset of the elements from XHTML Transitional, but does not include support for strictly presentational elements or elements that will not likely be included in future versions of XHTML. In the future, XHTML documents will separate presentation from content and use style sheets to define presentation formatting such as font types, colors, and styles. Use XHTML Strict with Cascading Style Sheets (CSS). You will learn about CSS and how to use style sheets with XHTML documents in Chapter Seven.

```
<!DOCTYPE html
       PUBLIC "-//W3C//DTD XHTML 1.0 Strict//EN"
       "http://www.w3.org/TR/xhtml1/DTD/xhtml1-strict.dtd">
```

On the Web: http://www.w3.org/TR/xhtml1/DTD/xhtml1-strict.dtd

Figure 1.3 The Three Versions of the XHTML 1.0 Specification

Our First XHTML Document

We'll begin our example by examining the document we would like to mark up with formatting elements. Figure 1.4 is a course description written as a plain text document with no information added for formatting:

```
Course Name: Introduction to XHTML
Course Number: CS 112
Instructor: T. Perdue
Meeting Time: Wednesday, 5:30pm-7:30pm

Course Description: This course covers the basics of how to
write XHTML Web documents.

Prerequsites: CS 101—Introduction to Computers, CS 103—
Introduction to Web Site Design, CS 110—Designing Web Pages
with HTML
```

Figure 1.4 Unformatted Text Document

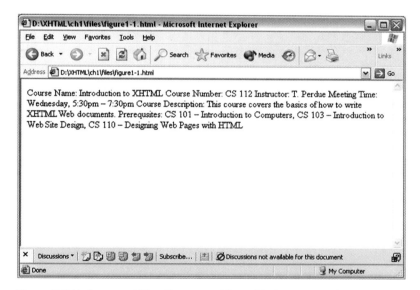

Figure 1.5 Unformatted Text Document Viewed in Internet Explorer

Figure 1.5 shows how this plain text document looks when viewed in Internet Explorer. As you can see, the Web browser can open the document, but without formatting instructions, it does not know how to correctly format this document. Web browsers ignore all whitespace characters, including line breaks, so without the proper markup, this document displays as just a block of text.

HTML Document

Now, we'll add some formatting elements to the document. We will create this document in both HTML (Figure 1.6) and XHTML (Figure 1.8), and then examine the differences between the two.

```
1   <HTML>                                          The document starts with an opening tag for the HTML element.
2     <HEAD>
3       <TITLE>Introduction to XHTML</TITLE>        This is followed by the header section
4     </HEAD>                                        and the title of the document.
5     <BODY>
6       <STRONG>Course Name:</STRONG>   Introduction to XHTML <BR>
7       <STRONG>Course Number:</STRONG>   CS 112 <BR>
8       <STRONG>Instructor: </STRONG> T. Perdue </BR>
9       <STRONG>Meeting Time: </STRONG>  Wednesday, 5:30pm-7:30pm <BR>
10      <P>
11      <STRONG>Course Description: </STRONG> This course covers the
            basics of how to write XHTML Web documents.
12      <P>
13      <STRONG>Prerequsites: </STRONG>               The main body of
14      <UL>                                          the document
15        <LI>CS 101-Introduction to Computers        contains a mix of
16        <LI>CS 103-Introduction to Web Site Design  markup elements
17        <LI>CS 110-Designing Web Pages with HTML    and content.
18      </UL>
19    </BODY>
20  </HTML>                                          The document always ends with the closing tag for the HTML element.
```

Figure 1.6 HTML Document

☆ **SHORTCUT Instructions for Doing This Example Yourself**

1. Open a text editor on your computer, like Notepad in Windows or SimpleText on a Macintosh.
2. Type in the HTML code from the example and save the document as `example1.html`. Do not include the line numbers.
3. Open your browser and click on the File menu.
4. Click on the Open or Open Page menu item and choose the file `example1.html`, which you saved in step 2.

The page will then be displayed in your browser.

After adding HTML elements to our document, we can use a Web browser to open and display the document with the formatting styles applied. As you can see in Figure 1.7, the document now contains formatting, as described by the HTML. Notice that the beginning and ending tags for the HTML element, `<HTML>` and `</HTML>` on lines 1 and 20, enclose the entire document.

XHTML Document

Now, let's create the same document in XHTML in Figure 1.8.

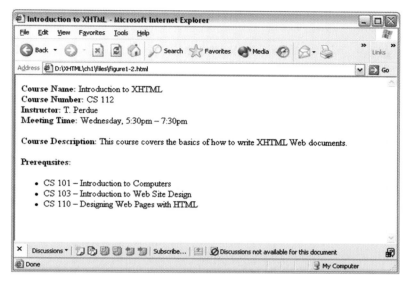

Figure 1.7 HTML Document Viewed in Internet Explorer

```
1   <?xml version="1.0"?>                          Begin with XHTML document headings.
2   <!DOCTYPE html PUBLIC "-//W3C//DTD XHTML 1.0 Strict//EN"
       "http://www.w3.org/TR/xhtml1/DTD/xhtml1-strict.dtd">
3   <html xmlns="http://www.w3.org/1999/xhtml">     The document starts with an opening
4   <head>                                          tag for the <html> element.
5      <title>Introduction to XHTML</title>         This is followed by the header section
6   </head>                                         and the title of the document.
7   <body>
8      <strong>Course Name:</strong>  Introduction to XHTML <br />
9      <strong>Course Number: </strong>  CS 112 <br />
10     <strong>Instructor: </strong> Tabitha Perdue <br />
11     <strong>Meeting Time: </strong>  Wednesday, 5:30pm-7:30pm <br />
12     <p />
13     <strong>Course Description: </strong> This course covers the
          basics of how to write XHTML Web documents.
14     <p />                                         The main body of
15     <strong>Prerequsites: </strong>              the document
16     <ul>                                          contains a mix of
17        <li>CS 101-Introduction to Computers </li> markup elements
18        <li>CS 103-Introduction to Web Site Design </li> and content.
19        <li>CS 110-Designing Web Pages with HTML </li>
20     </ul>
21  </body>
22  </html>        The document ends with a closing tag for the <html> element.
```

Figure 1.8 XHTML Document

You may notice some differences in the code between the HTML and XHTML documents—these are discussed in the next section. One difference is the addition of the XML and DOCTYPE declarations in the XHTML document. Again, the XML declaration is optional in XHTML but including it is highly recommended. The DOCTYPE declaration was optional in HTML documents but is required for XHTML documents. Despite the differences, if you view the XHTML document in a Web browser, it will look identical to the HTML document in Figure 1.7.

Differences Between XHTML and HTML

Looking at the two examples, you probably noticed that the code is very similar. Both HTML and XHTML are platform- and vendor-independent. Both use elements and tags to describe pieces of data within a document. As mentioned earlier, they use the same set of element names based on the element set from HTML 4. However, XHTML has much stricter syntax and is more powerful and flexible than HTML. Following are some of the major differences between XHTML and HTML:

1. XHTML documents contain the XML and DOCTYPE declarations at the top of the document. The XML declaration is optional but the DOCTYPE declaration is required. The DOCTYPE declaration was optional in HTML. These are lines 1 and 2 in the XHTML example. We cover this in detail later in this chapter.

2. XHTML documents must be well formed, meaning that they need to adhere to the syntax rules for the language. HTML, however, does not strictly require that documents be well formed. This is covered later in this chapter.

3. XHTML is not dependent on a single document type or set of markup elements, like HTML. XHTML can be extended or used in conjunction with other markup languages.

4. Element and attribute names must be lowercase. XHTML elements and attributes are case sensitive, while HTML elements and attributes are not. In our examples, notice that the HTML elements are all uppercase: `<HTML>`, `<STRONG>`, `</BODY>`. This was done simply as a matter of style. These tags could have been written in lowercase or in a combination of upper and lowercase, and HTML would still have interpreted them correctly: `<html>`, `<Strong>`, `</BoDy>`. The XHTML document, on the other hand, must have all of its tags and attributes in lowercase.

5. For nonempty elements, XHTML requires end tags. An empty element is an element that does not contain an end tag. This is not a requirement for HTML, as the HTML element set contains a subset of elements that do not have end tags. In our example, the `<BR>` and `<P>` HTML elements are empty elements. In the XHTML code, notice that these elements are written a little differently: `<br />` and `<p />`. In XHTML, all elements must either have an end tag or end in `/>`.

6. Attribute values must always be quoted in XHTML. This was not a requirement in HTML. The following is valid in HTML:

```
<img src=picture.gif>
```

The attribute `src` has a value of `picture.gif` assigned to it. However, the same line in the XHTML example places quotes around the value of the attribute:

```
<img src="picture.gif" />
```

The W3C provides a great deal of information about the differences between HTML and XHTML. Links where you can get more information about the differences and compatibility issues with current Web browsers are provided at the end of the chapter.

◎◎ Rules and Tools for Building XHTML Documents

Writing Well-Formed XHTML Documents

Because XHTML is an XML application, you must adhere to the same syntax rules as any in XML language. If you are used to writing HTML code, these rules may seem a bit intimidating, as HTML does not force developers to adhere so strictly to syntax rules. XHTML, however, is much more picky and will not allow code to be written improperly. An XHTML document that adheres to XML syntax rules is said to be well formed. A document that is not well formed will generate an error in a parser program.

Following are the syntax rules for writing well-formed XML documents:

1. All XHTML documents must contain the root element `<html>` and cannot contain more than one root element.

2. All elements must have a start and end tag, such as `<h1>.........</h1>`. The exception is an empty element, which must have a forward slash (/) before the end tag: `<br />`.

3. Elements must be nested properly and cannot overlap. Each element must be contained completely inside of its parent element. This rule is the same as for math functions. Here is an example:

```
( X * [Y + Z] )
```

Notice that there are two parts to this equation, one that is surrounded by the parentheses and the other by brackets (`[` and `]`). The subequation `[B + C]` is entirely contained within the outer equation, which is delineated by the parentheses. It is illegal to write the equation like this:

```
( X * [Y + Z ) ]
```

Here, the outer equation ends (with a parenthesis) before the inner one (with a bracket).

This same rule applies to nesting elements in XHTML. Here are examples of illegal and legal element nesting:

Illegal nesting of elements: `<h1><strong>......</h1></strong>`

In this example, the ending tags for `<h1>` and `<strong>` overlap. This is illegal in XHTML and will cause a parsing error.

Proper nesting of elements: `<h1><strong>......</strong></h1>`

Here, the `<strong>` element is correctly closed before the `<h1>` element.

4. All attributes must have a value, and that value must be enclosed in quotes. Both double and single quotes are allowed and can be nested, as long as you are consistent and you do not use the same type of quote twice. Here are some valid examples:

   Example using single quotes: `<img src='picture.gif'>`

   Example using double quotes: `<img src="picture.gif">`

   Example of using nested quotes: Double quotes surround the entire value of the attribute, and single quotes surround the string `"Starry Night"` within the value string: `<img src=" picture.gif" alt="Image of 'Starry Night' by Van Gogh">`

5. Attributes must be placed in the start tag of an element, and no attribute can appear more than once. Here is an example:

   `<a href="page2.html" href="page3.html">Click here</a>`

   In this example, the attribute name `href` appears twice, which is illegal in XHTML syntax.

6. Element names are case sensitive. For example, `<TITLE>` and `</title>` are both legal beginning and ending tags in HTML, because it is not case sensitive. In XHTML all tags must be lowercase so `<TITLE>` would produce an error.

☆**TIP**   **Adding Elements to XHTML**

As stated previously, you can add elements to the base XHTML element set if needed. There is no requirement that add-on element names must be in all lowercase, but keep in mind that the element names are case sensitive, so you must use the same case in both the beginning and ending tags.

Certain markup characters cannot appear in the content of an element. Examples include the < and > characters. XML recognizes these characters as starting and ending tags, and will get confused if you use these as part of the content of an element. You must use a character entity to represent this character as part of content.

☆**WARNING**   **XHTML Syntax Is More Strict than HTML Syntax**

If you are familiar with HTML, you will notice that XHTML is much stricter than HTML. HTML browsers, such as Internet Explorer and Netscape Navigator, are very forgiving of poorly written HTML code, and an HTML document that has errors will usually display fine in a browser window. The same is true for XHTML documents viewed in these browsers. The browsers will allow you to write XHTML code that is not well formed, but that would defeat the purpose of developing your pages in XHTML to be compatible with XML parsers in future browsers. Current browsers will not produce error messages if you have written code with errors, so always make sure to check your code with an XML or XHTML parser to make sure that it is well formed.

Well-Formed vs. Valid Documents

The terms *well-formed* and *valid* in reference to writing good XHTML are not the same. They are both very important pieces of developing code that will be compatible with future tools, but they are distinctively different in the kinds of errors they test for. A well-formed document, as you learned above, must adhere to a set of structural rules. These rules apply to the syntax of how the code is written, but does not pay attention to the code itself. For example, if you include names of elements or attributes that are not part of the HTML 4.01 specification, but you follow the syntax rules covered in the last section, your document will pass the well-formed test, even though you have used elements that are not part of the spec.

For a document to be valid, it must not only be well formed, but also conform to the rules of the DTD that it lists in its DOCTYPE declaration. The DTD contains the set of all valid element and attribute names that can be used for that document type. Following is the XHTML Transitional DTD:

```
<!DOCTYPE html
        PUBLIC "-//W3C//DTD XHTML 1.0 Transitional//EN"
        "http://www.w3.org/TR/xhtml1/DTD/xhtml1-transitional.dtd">
```

You can choose to store the DTD document on your local filesystem if you wish, putting it in `C:\dtd\xhtml1-transitional.dtd`. It does not matter where this DTD is stored, as long as the validating parser program you are using can get to the document to validate against it. Following is the DOCTYPE declaration that references the DTD on the local filesystem:

```
<!DOCTYPE html
        PUBLIC "-//W3C//DTD XHTML 1.0 Transitional//EN"
        "C:\dtd\xhtml1-transitional.dtd ">
```

XHTML Editors

Because XHTML documents are plain text documents, you can use any text-editing program, such as Notepad on Windows computers and SimpleText on Macintosh computers, to write your XHTML pages. However, this process can be tedious and prone to errors. If you are going to write your pages by hand, you should always check them with a parser.

There are literally hundreds of programs available that you can use to write your pages. Some of these programs are free—all you need to do is download them from the Internet and install them. Of the rest, most have demo versions that you can download and try for free for 30 days. Free or not, most have features that will check your code.

The W3C supports an editor called Amaya, which is an Open Source project. Amaya is both an editing program and a browser. This program can be downloaded for free from the Web. There is a link at the end of this chapter to the Web site where you can download Amaya. You can also refer to this book's website for a list of both free and commercial editors.

Parsers

In order to display XHTML documents with formatting, you need a program that knows what the elements are and how to display them correctly. This kind of program is called a **parser** because it "parses" through the text of the document looking for markup elements. Web browsers contain a parser for HTML and XHTML documents that will scan through documents looking for markup elements in order to display the Web page with the correct formatting. However, the parsers contained in most Web browsers are not strict and will allow for poorly written code. A Web page that does not follow the syntax rules described above may not be well formed or valid but may still show up fine in a Web browser.

In order to verify that your document is well formed and valid, you need a parser that checks your XHTML document to ensure that you have followed the rules and that your documents are well formed. There are two kinds of parsers: validating and nonvalidating. A nonvalidating parser will read your document and look for syntax errors according to the language rules covered above. A validating parser will check your document against a DTD. If there are errors in your document, the parser will display an error message and many times will even tell you where in the document the error is located.

Validating Our XHTML Document

Using the W3C Online Markup Validation Service

Let's check our XHTML document from Figure 1.8 to see whether it is well formed and valid. There are many free and commercial programs that will check your documents. For this example, we'll use a free online validating tool from the W3C Web site. It can check your pages either from your computer or from a Web site. Figure 1.9 is the Web site, which is located at `http://validator.w3.org`.

Figure 1.10 shows the results of testing our document. According to this site, our document is both well formed and valid.

Let's see what happens when a page with errors is tested. Let's change our document so that it is *not* well formed and valid, and test it again. We'll make the highlighted changes so we get Figure 1.11:

1. Remove the end `</title>` tag from line 5.

2. Remove the empty element terminator from the `<br />` element on line 8.

3. Add an attribute to the `<strong>` element on line 15 called `attribute`. This attribute is not part of the DTD for the `<strong>` element.

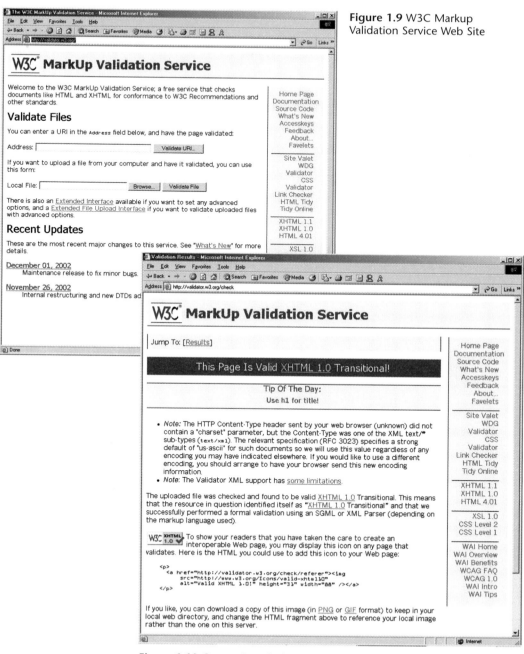

Figure 1.9 W3C Markup Validation Service Web Site

Figure 1.10 Course Description Document Results After Being Validated

```
1   <?xml version="1.0"?>
2   <!DOCTYPE html PUBLIC "-//W3C//DTD XHTML 1.0 Transitional//EN"
       "http://www.w3.org/TR/xhtml1/DTD/xhtml1-transitional.dtd">
3    <html xmlns="http://www.w3.org/1999/xhtml">
4    <head>
5       <title>Introduction to XHTML
6    </head>
7    <body>
8       <strong>Course Name:</strong>   Introduction to XHTML <br>
9       <strong>Course Number: </strong>   CS 112 <br />
10      <strong>Instructor: </strong> Tabitha Perdue <br />
11      <strong>Meeting Time: </strong>  Wednesday, 5:30pm-7:30pm <br />
12      <p />
13      <strong>Course Description: </strong> This course covers the
          basics of how to write XHTML Web documents.
14      <p />
15      <strong attribute="yes">Prerequistes: </strong>
16      <ul>
17         <li>CS 101-Introduction to Computers </li>
18         <li>CS 103-Introduction to Web Site Design </li>
19         <li>CS 110-Designing Web Pages with HTML </li>
20      </ul>
21    </body>
22 </html>
```

Figure 1.11 Course Description Document with Errors

Figure 1.12 shows the results of testing this code in the validator tool. As you can see, it picked out all of our errors.

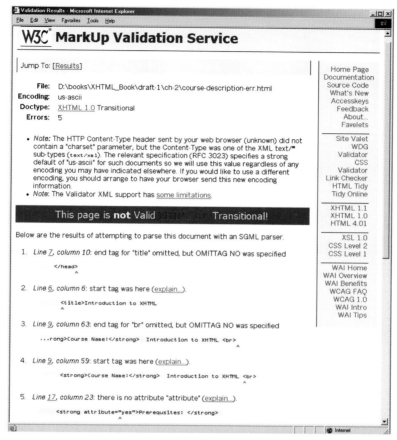

Figure 1.12 Course Description Document with Errors as Shown in Internet Explorer

☆ Summary

▷ Standards for Web technologies are managed by an organization called the World Wide Web Consortium, or the W3C.

▷ The Web is built using a client-server model.

▷ SGML is the predecessor to current markup languages, including XHTML, HTML, and XML.

▷ XHTML is an XML application.

▷ XHTML is being developed as the successor to HTML in response to the limitations of HTML.

▷ XHTML syntax is stricter than HTML syntax.

▷ Although XHTML and HTML use the same element set, there are differences between them.

☆ Online References

World Wide Web Consortium XML Web site
`http://www.w3c.org/XML`

HTML and XHTML homepage (on the W3C Web site)
`http://www.w3.org/MarkUp`

HTML 4.01 recommendation (on the W3C Web site)
`http://www.w3.org/TR/html401`

XHTML 1.0 recommendation (on the W3C Web site)
`http://www.w3.org/TR/xhtml1`

XHTML overview
`http://hotwired.lycos.com/webmonkey/00/50/index2a.html`

W3C documentation of differences between XHTML and HTML 4
`http://www.w3.org/TR/xhtml1/#diffs`

List of XHTML editors
`http://www.chughes.com/xhtml`

☆ Review Questions

1. What is a markup language?

2. What are a few reasons why it is important to have a cross-platform, vendor-independent file format like HTML and XHTML?

3. What are some limitations of HTML?

4. List three differences between HTML and XHTML.

5. List two advantages of XHTML over HTML.

☆ Hands-On Exercises

1. Go to the W3C Web site and locate the most recent XHTML recommendation.

2. The W3C Web site on markup languages (`http://www.w3.org/MarkUp`) lists the current and new specifications being developed around XHTML. Go to this site and research two XHTML technologies being developed.

3. Create and save the HTML and XHTML documents for the Course Description example in this chapter and view them in a Web browser. Refer to the instructions provided in the Shortcut box for the example with details of how to create, save, and view the documents.

4. Create an XHTML document for the following:

   ```
   Boating Gear List
   The following is a list of items that are essential
   on any boat trip:
   1. Life Jackets
   2. Sun tan lotion
   3. Cold drinks
   4. Bathing suits
   5. Compass
   ```

5. View the documents you just created in a Web browser and validate your code using the W3C validator page.

CHAPTER TWO

Basic Formatting and Hypertext Links

This chapter covers the fundamentals of XHTML, including document structure and many formatting elements. Learning correct structure and syntax is crucial in learning how to create XHTML documents. By the end of this chapter, you will have a solid understanding of how documents are structured and how to perform basic formatting using XHTML elements.

Chapter Objectives

- ☆ Explain the three parts of an XHTML document
- ☆ Describe the elements that make up the framework of an XHTML document
- ☆ Introduce block-level and character-level formatting elements
- ☆ Describe the three types of XHTML lists

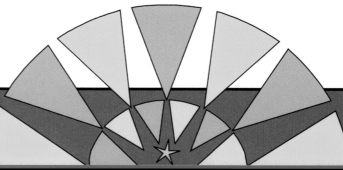

◎◎ How XHTML Documents Are Structured

The Three Parts of an XHTML Document

XHTML documents are comprised of a simple three-part framework:

1. Document prolog
2. Header section
3. Body of document

Figure 2.1 shows a basic document framework for XHTML Strict. Even though XHTML has three versions, we focus on the Strict version because it most closely resembles the future of XHTML. The elements we cover appear in all three versions, but the Transitional and Frameset versions contain a few elements and attributes that are being phased out of the XHTML language and are only included in Transitional and Frameset for backward compatibility with older versions of HTML.

☆**TIP**   **Refer to DTD for Element and Attribute Details**

We will cover most of the elements and attributes that are part of the XHTML Strict specification, but we don't have space to cover every detail. Refer to the DTD in Appendix A or the W3C Web site for more information about the elements and attributes for each of the three flavors of XHTML.

```
1    <?xml version="1.0"?>                      The document prolog declarations.
2    <!DOCTYPE html PUBLIC "-//W3C//DTD XHTML 1.0 Strict//EN"
         "http://www.w3.org/TR/xhtml1/DTD/xhtml1-strict.dtd">
3    <html xmlns="http://www.w3.org/1999/xhtml">    The <html>
4      <head>                                         root element.
5        <title>Strict XHTML Document</title>       Header
6      </head>                                       information
7      <body>
8        <!-- Body of document goes here -->
9      </body>                    Open and close <body> tags, between which
10   </html>                      the main body of the document is contained.
```

Figure 2.1 XHTML Strict Document Framework

Document Framework Elements

The elements that make up the framework of XHTML documents do not produce any output in a browser window. Instead they provide information to the program about the document.

The `<html>` Element

The `<html>` element is the **root element** of an XHTML document, within which every other element in the document is contained. The document begins with the

<html> start tag and ends with the </html> closing tag. The header and body information of the document are contained in the root element.

As you probably noticed in the examples in Figure 2.1, the opening <html> tag defines an attribute called xmlns with a value of http://www.w3.org/1999/xhtml. This attribute declares the XHTML namespace, is required of all XHTML documents, and is inserted into a document by a parsing program even if you do not include it in your code. See the TIP box on this page for more information about this attribute.

> ☆ **TIP** **A Word About Namespaces**
>
> The opening <html> tag has an attribute called xmlns, which has a value of http://www.w3.org/1999/xhtml. The xmlns attribute stands for XML Namespace, and the value of this attribute defines the namespace that the element names for XHTML belong to. Namespaces in XML are collections of element and attribute names for particular document types. Even though XHTML has a predefined set of element and attribute names, XML allows you to create your own language and your own element and attribute names. This can lead to confusion if your language element and/or attribute names are the same as someone else's names but have different meanings. Namespaces in XML allow you to specify which namespace the element and attribute names belong to. The xmlns attribute tells the program parsing the document that the elements and attribute names contained within the <html> element belong to the XHTML namespace.
>
> The value of the xmlns attribute, http://www.w3.org/1999/xhtml, resembles a Web address but is simply used to uniquely identify the namespace. If you go to this page on the Internet, you will find an informational page provided by the W3C. This is not required of name-space values, it is simply a courtesy provided by the W3C. The xmlns attribute for the <html> element is required for XHTML documents and is specified as a fixed value in each of the three XHTML DTDs. You can safely omit the attribute from your <html> start tag if you want to, because the parsing program will add it automatically, but we recommend that you include it.

The <head> Element

The opening <head> tag comes directly after the <html> opening tag in an XHTML document. This element must be placed inside the <html> element; it contains information about the document that is mainly used by programs, such as keywords for search engines and link information that defines the relationship this document has to other documents. It also contains the required <title> element. Following are the elements that the <head> element can contain. All but the <title> element are optional:

☆ <title>—Defines the title of the document.

☆ <base>—Defines the document's base URL, which is used for relative links in the document.

☆ <link>—Defines the relationship of this document to other documents.

☆ <meta>—Defines additional information about the document, including the document's content type and special instructions for browsers and search engines.

☆ <script>—Defines links to scripts used with the document, such as JavaScript.

☆ `<style>`—Defines links to style sheets to be used with the document, such as Cascading Style Sheets, covered in Chapter Three.

The `<title>` Element

The `<title>` element is required and must be contained within the open and close tags of the `<head>` element. There can only be one `<title>` element per document. It defines the title of the document that is displayed in the title bar of browser windows as well as the name of bookmarks to that page. Most search engines use the content of the `<title>` element as the text to display on their results pages as well. Figure 2.2 shows the title bar of Internet Explorer displaying the content of the `<title>`.

`<title>This is my title</title>`

Figure 2.2 The `<title>` Element Displayed in Internet Explorer's Title Bar

The `<body>` Element

The `<body>` element contains the content and all of the markup elements of the document. The body of the document is contained between the open and end `<body>` tags. All of the other elements that you will learn about in the remainder of this book are contained within the `<body>` element.

☆**WARNING** **Formatting Elements in XHTML**

Previous versions of HTML included various formatting attributes that would allow you to set the background color for the document and define text attributes in the body element, such as `bgcolor`. XHTML Strict uses style sheets to define these formatting attributes, so they are not included in the specification. If you are using XHTML Transitional or Frameset, you can include additional formatting attributes with the `<body>` element.

Many of the elements covered here have additional attributes that can be used with XHTML Transitional and Frameset. We include these attributes and which version they are compatible with where appropriate, but please refer to the specifications for each version for more information.

Style attributes (used only with XHTML Transitional and Frameset, not Strict):

☆ `bgcolor`—Used to set the background color of the document.

☆ `text`—Used to set the color of the text of the document.

☆ `link`—Used to set the color for hyperlinks. The default color for links is blue.

☆ vlink—Used to set the color for hyperlinks that have been followed by the user.

☆ alink—Used to set the color for hyperlinks that are currently being activated.

(Refer to the Web-Safe Colors chart on the last page of the book for color values.)

⊚☉ Basic Formatting Elements

Now that you understand how XHTML documents are structured, let's start building some Web pages. We'll start with basic formatting elements (Figure 2.3), show you examples of how to use each of the elements, and create a few documents to show you how they look in a Web browser.

Element Name	Formatting Style
<p> ...</p>	Paragraph element
 	Line break
<h1>...</h1> to <h6>...</h6>	Heading elements (1 is largest, 6 is smallest)
<hr />	Horizontal rule
<div>...</div>	Section divider

Figure 2.3 Block-level Elements Summary Chart

Documents are broken into logical sections based on the document content to make it easier for users to read. The elements described in this section are used to break documents into logical chunks and to label the main content headings. These elements are referred to as **block-level elements** because they describe blocks of content.

The <p> *Element*

The <p> element divides content into paragraphs. The <p> tag designates the beginning of a paragraph, and the </p> tag ends the paragraph. Most browsers will automatically insert a double carriage return around the paragraph element.

<p>This is a very short paragraph.</p>

The
 Element

The <br /> element is the **line break element**. Similar to the <p> element, it is used to break up sections of text. The <br /> element causes the browser to create a single carriage return. The <br /> element is an empty element and must end with /> in order to conform to the rules of a well-formed document.

This paragraph has a line <br /> separated by a line break.

The `<h1>` ... `<h6>` Elements

These elements are the **heading elements**. They are used to label section headings of a document. There are six heading levels: `<h1>`, `<h2>`, `<h3>`, `<h4>`, `<h5>`, and `<h6>`. The `<h1>` head should be used to label the top-most heading, and the rest of the elements should be used for subheads, much like a table of contents hierarchy. The browser will display the font for each of the levels differently, starting with a larger font size for `<h1>` and progressively getting smaller as the heading number increases.

```
<h1>This is a level 1 heading.</h1>
<h2>This is a level 2 heading.</h2>
<h3>This is a level 3 heading.</h3>
<h4>This is a level 4 heading.</h4>
<h5>This is a level 5 heading.</h5>
<h6>This is a level 6 heading.</h6>
```

The `<hr />` Element

The `<hr />` is the **horizontal rule element**, used to create a visible horizontal line on the Web page to indicate a section break.

```
There is a horizontal rule line between this line <hr />
and this line.
```

XHTML Transitional and Frameset provide a set of attributes that can be used with this element to customize the rule:

The `<div>` Element

The `<div>` element is used to divide sections of content. This element is used to label sections of the document, and can contain any number of other elements. This element can use the `id` and `class` core XHTML attributes to identify the various sections of the document to be used with parser programs.

```
<div>This is a section </div>
```

Examples

Let's look at an example using the framework and formatting elements we just learned. Figure 2.4 shows the code and Figure 2.5 shows the document as it would display in Internet Explorer.

```
1   <?xml version="1.0"?>
2   <!DOCTYPE html PUBLIC "-//W3C//DTD XHTML 1.0 Strict//EN"
        "http://www.w3.org/TR/xhtml1/DTD/xhtml1-strict.dtd">
3   <html xmlns="http://www.w3.org/1999/xhtml">
4       <head>
5           <title>XHTML Block-level Elements</title>
6       </head>
7       <body>
8           <p> This is a paragraph about African Gray
               parrots. The African Gray is one of the most
```

```
     popular pet birds of the parrot family. It is
     known for its intellegence and is one of the best
     talkers of all domesticated birds. This parrot is
     native to Africa and can live to be almost 70
     years old.</p>
9    <div> This is also a paragraph about African Gray
     parrots. Here is some additional information about
     the African Gray parrot separated by line breaks:
     (break here) <br />The African Gray parrot is
     about 15 inches long and (break here) <br />has a
     wing span of about 20 inches.</div>
10   <hr />
11       <h1>This is a level 1 heading</h1>
12       <h2>This is a level 2 heading</h2>
13       <h3>This is a level 3 heading</h3>
14       <h4>This is a level 4 heading</h4>
15       <h5>This is a level 5 heading</h5>
16       <h6>This is a level 6 heading</h6>
17   <hr />
18 </body>
19 </html>
```

Figure 2.4 Block-level Elements Example

Figure 2.5 Block-level Elements Example in Internet Explorer

Presentational Text Formatting

Text formatting elements are referred to as **character-level elements** because, unlike the block-level elements, which describe blocks of content, these elements describe the text itself. Character-level elements describe the formatting of words or phrases as opposed to sections or paragraphs.

The first text-formatting elements we cover are **presentational styles** for formatting text. Presentational styles describe how the text should be displayed, in bold type or italics for example. Figure 2.6 lists the most commonly used presentational elements.

Element Name	Formatting Style
`<b> ...</b>`	Bold font style
`<big>...</big>`	Increases current font size
`<i>...</i>`	Italic font style
`<small>...</small>`	Decreases current font size
`<sub>...</sub>`	Subscripted text
`<sup>...</sup>`	Superscripted text

Figure 2.6 Presentational Text Formatting Elements

Example

Figure 2.7 shows an XHTML document that uses presentational elements. Figure 2.8 shows how this document looks in Internet Explorer.

```
1   <?xml version="1.0"?>
2   <!DOCTYPE html PUBLIC "-//W3C//DTD XHTML 1.0 Strict//EN"
        "http://www.w3.org/TR/xhtml1/DTD/xhtml1-strict.dtd">
3   <html xmlns="http://www.w3.org/1999/xhtml">
4       <head>
5           <title>XHTML Presentational Text Formatting
            Elements</title>
6       </head>
7       <body>
8           <p>
9               This text is formatted in <b>bold</b>.
10          </p>
11          <p>
12              This text is formatted in <i>italics</i>.
13          </p>
```

```
14        <p>
15            See how <big>the big element</big> increases
              the current font size and how <small>the small
              element</small>decreases it.
16        </p>
17        <p>
18            This is how the <sup>superscript element</sup>
              and the element <sub>subscript element</sub>
              format text.
19        </p>
20      </body>
21 </html>
```

Figure 2.7 Presentational Text Formatting Elements

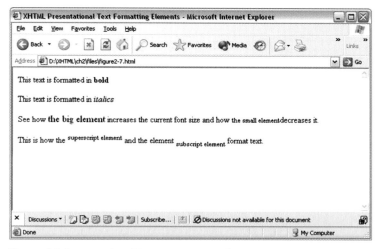

Figure 2.8 Presentational Text Formatting Elements in Internet Explorer

Logical Text Formatting

The second set of text-formatting elements we will cover are **logical styles** for formatting text. Logical styles describe the meaning of the style more than the actual format. Initially, browsers were left to determine the presentation of these tags as they saw fit, but over the years certain standards developed, and these are unlikely to change in the foreseeable future. For example, if you want a certain type, like bold, you should use the <b> element, but the <strong> element will give you the same effect. Figure 2.9 lists the most commonly used logical elements.

Element Name	Formatting Style
`<cite> ...</cite>`	Defines a citation.
`<code>...</code>`	Presents computer code examples.
`<em>...</em>`	Emphasis. In most browsers, this is italics.
`<strong>...</strong>`	Emphasis. In most browsers, this is bold.

Figure 2.9 Logical Text Formatting Elements

Example

Figure 2.10 is an XHTML document that uses presentational elements. Figure 2.11 shows how this document looks in Internet Explorer.

```
1   <?xml version="1.0"?>
2   <!DOCTYPE html PUBLIC "-//W3C//DTD XHTML 1.0 Strict//EN"
        "http://www.w3.org/TR/xhtml1/DTD/xhtml1-strict.dtd">
3   <html xmlns="http://www.w3.org/1999/xhtml">
4       <head>
5           <title>XHTML Logical Text Formatting Elements</title>
6       </head>
7       <body>
8           <p>
9               Following is a citation: <br />
10              <cite>
11                  Four score and seven years ago our fathers brought
                    forth on this continent, a new nation, conceived in
                    Liberty, and dedicated to the proposition that all
                    men are created equal.
12              </cite>
13          </p>
14          <p>
15              Following is a block of code: <br />
16              <code>
17                  while ($x &lt; 10) { <br />
18                      $var = $x + 1; <br />
19                      $count++; <br />
20                  } <br />
21              </code>
22          </p>
23          <p>
24              This text is formatted using the <strong>strong
                element</strong>
25          </p>
26          <p>
27              This text is formatted using the <em>em element</em>
```

```
28          </p>
29        </body>
30  </html>
```

Figure 2.10 Logical Text Formatting Elements

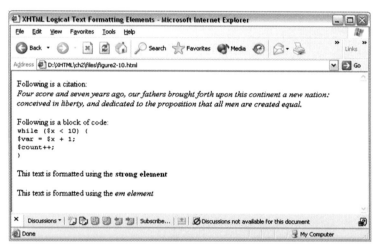

Figure 2.11 Logical Text Formatting Elements in Internet Explorer

⭐**TIP**   **Character Entities in XHTML**

The character for the less than symbol on line 17 is written as <. Certain characters in XHTML have special meaning to parsers, like less than < and greater than >. These characters identify the beginning and end of a tag, so if you want to add these characters as their literal values, you must use the **character entity code** for them. A character entity is written in the following syntax: &code;. It begins with an ampersand (&) character, then the code for the entity, then a semicolon (;).

Hundreds of symbols can be referenced and included on Web pages using entities. Some of the more popular symbols can be referenced by their abbreviations, like less than (lt) and greater than (gt), but they also can be referenced using their decimal value in the ASCII table. Below are a few character entities. You'll find links to more character entity lists at the end of this chapter.

Symbol	Description	XHTML Code
>	Greater than	> or &62;
<	Less than	< or &60;
(r)	Trademark	™ or &174;
(c)	Copyright	© or &169;
¢	Cent sign	¢ or &162;

 XHTML Lists

XHTML provides three main types of lists: numbered, bulleted, and definition. Each of these list types, shown in Figure 2.12, is covered in this section.

List Type	Element	Item Element
Ordered list	`<ol>...</ol>`	`<li>...</li>`
Unordered list	`<ul>...</ul>`	`<li>...</li>`
Definition list	`<dl>...</dl>`	`<dt>...</dt>`, `<dd>...</dd>`

Figure 2.12 XHTML List Elements

Ordered Lists

Ordered lists are numbered and are contained within the `<ol>`, **ordered list**, element. The list begins with the start tag for `<ol>`, may have any number of `<li>`, **list items**, and ends with the closing `</ol>` tag. The browser will list each of the elements in a numbered sequential list. Following is an example of an ordered list:

```
<p>The Lord of the Rings Trilogy</p>
<ol>
    <li>The Fellowship of the Rings</li>
    <li>The Two Towers</li>
    <li>The Return of the King</li>
</ol>
```

Ordered lists can be formatted with two attributes. The `start` attribute sets the starting number in the list to be something other than the default value of 1. The `type` attribute identifies the type of numbering to use. The default numbering for `<ol>` lists is "1, 2, 3..." The values of `type` can be one of the following:

1—The default setting. Arabic numbers (1, 2, 3...)

A—Uppercase letters (A, B, C...)

a—Lowercase letters (a, b, c...)

I—Roman numerals (I, II, III...)

i—Small Roman numerals (i, ii, iii...)

Unordered Lists

Unordered lists are bulleted instead of numbered. The list begins with the open `<ul>`, **unordered list**, tag, followed by any number of `<li>` elements, and ending with the closing `</ul>` tag. Following is an example of an unordered list:

```
<p>College Sports</p>
<ul>
    <li>Football</li>
    <li>Basketball</li>
    <li>Hockey</li>
</ul>
```

Ordered lists only have one attribute, `type`. The possible values for `type` for unordered lists are `disc`, `square`, and `circle`.

Definition Lists

Definition lists are lists of terms and their definitions. They are a little different than ordered and unordered lists in that the items are listed in pairs. The `<dl>` and `</dl>` tags surround the list. The name of the term appears between `<dt>` and `</dt>`, and the definition is between `<dd>` and `</dd>`. Following is an example of a definition list:

```
<dl>
    <dt>Term 1</dt>
    <dd>Definition 1</dd>
    <dt>Term 2</dt>
    <dd>Definition 2</dd>
    <dt>Term 3</dt>
    <dd> Definition 3</dd>
</dl>
```

Nesting Lists

Nesting lists include one list within another list. Lists can be nested any number of times, and list types can be mixed. Following is an example of an ordered list and an unordered list with a nested ordered list. Notice how the symbols for the bullets change for the nested list. Also notice that the ending `</li>` tag comes after the end of the nested list for the items that have nested lists.

```
<ul>
    <li>Favorite Football Teams
        <ul>
            <li>New England Patriots</li>
            <li>Tennessee Titans</li>
            <li>Dallas Cowboys</li>
        </ul>
    </li>
    <li>Favorite Players
        <ol>
            <li>Tom Brady - Patriots</li>
            <li>Steve McNair - Titans</li>
            <li>Adam Vinitari - Patriots</li>
            <li>Eddie George - Titans</li>
        </ol>
    </li>
</ul>
```

Example

Following is an example using list elements. Figure 2.13 demonstrates the list elements and their attributes. Figure 2.14 shows the document as it would appear in Internet Explorer.

```
1    <?xml version="1.0"?>
2    <!DOCTYPE html PUBLIC "-//W3C//DTD XHTML 1.0 Strict//EN"
         "http://www.w3.org/TR/xhtml1/DTD/xhtml1-strict.dtd">
3    <html xmlns="http://www.w3.org/1999/xhtml">
4        <head>
5            <title>XHTML List Examples</title>
6        </head>
7        <body>
8            <h2>Ordered List Example</h2>
9            <!-- Ordered List Example -->
10           <h2>The Lord of the Rings Trilogy</h2>
11           <ol>
12               <li>The Fellowship of the Rings</li>
13               <li>The Two Towers</li>
14               <li>The Return of the King</li>
15           </ol>
16           <!-- Unordered List Example -->
17           <h2>Subway Lines in Boston</h2>
18           <ul>
19               <li>Blue Line</li>
20               <li>Green Line</li>
21               <li>Orange Line</li>
22               <li>Red Line</li>
23           </ul>
24           <!-- Definition List Example -->
25           <h2>Web Protocol Definitions</h2>
26           <dl>
27               <dt>HTTP</dt>
28               <dd>HyperText Transfer Protocol</dd>
29               <dt>FTP</dt>
30               <dd>File Transfer Protocol</dd>
31               <dt>XML</dt>
32               <dd>Extensible Markup Language</dd>
33           </dl>
34           <!-- Nested List Example -->
35           <h2>Football Favorites</h2>
36           <ul>
37               <li>Favorite Football Teams
38                   <ul>
39                       <li>New England Patriots</li>
40                       <li>Tennessee Titans</li>
41                       <li>Dallas Cowboys</li>
```

```
42                    </ul>
43                </li>
44                <li>Favorite Players
45                    <ol>
46                        <li>Tom Brady - Patriots</li>
47                        <li>Steve McNair - Titans</li>
48                        <li>Adam Vinitari - Patriots</li>
49                        <li>Eddie George - Titans</li>
50                    </ol>
51                </li>
51            </ul>
52        </body>
53  </html>
```

Figure 2.13 XHTML Lists

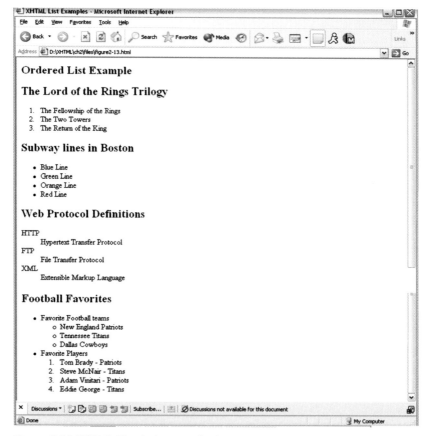

Figure 2.14 XHTML Lists in Internet Explorer

◎◎ Hypertext Links

What Is a Hypertext Link?

A **hypertext link**, or **hyperlink**, is an object in a Web page that when clicked on will redirect the browser to another Web page or file. Usually, hyperlinks take the form of blue, underlined text, or an image. Special linking elements are included in the HTML and XHTML specifications that allow Web page authors to use images or text within a Web page to create these links to other resources. The resource being linked to by the hyperlink is called the **target resource**. In addition to other Web pages, the target resource of a hyperlink can be an image file, a multimedia file (such as an audio or video file), another section within the same page, or any Web page or file anywhere on the Internet. Links provide Web page authors with a powerful means of organizing information and allow them to create very complex, cross-referenced Web sites with clickable tables of contents and menus.

Creating Links with the <a> Element

The <a> or **anchor element** in XHTML is used to create hyperlinks. These links require the user to perform an action—usually clicking on the link—in order for that link to do anything. The clickable region of the link can consist of text or images. If the user never clicks the linked image or text, the link is never activated. Following is the syntax of an anchor element:

```
<a href="http://chughes.com/index.html">This is a link.</a>
```

The text "This is a link" would be the clickable area of this link in a Web browser. The value of the `href` attribute is the URL of the file being linked to, or the target resource, which is `http://chughes.com/index.html`.

Let's look at how the anchor element is used. Figure 2.15 is an XHTML page that contains a number of links. Figure 2.16 shows the Web page in Internet Explorer.

```
1    <?xml version="1.0"?>
2    <!DOCTYPE html PUBLIC "-//W3C//DTD XHTML 1.0 Strict//EN"
         "http://www.w3.org/TR/xhtml1/DTD/xhtml1-strict.dtd">
3    <html xmlns="http://www.w3.org/1999/xhtml">
4      <head>
5        <title>Link Examples in XHTML</title>
6      </head>
7      <body>
8        <p>Here are some examples of links in XHTML:</p>
9        <p>
10           <a href="http://chughes.com/newpage.html">
             This is an absolute link to a new page.</a>
```

This link uses an **absolute** URL (`http://chughes.com/newpage.html`), meaning that the entire URL, including the protocol (`http://`) and domain name (`chughes.com`), has been included in the value for the `href` attribute.

```
12          </p>
13          <p>
```
> This link uses a **relative** URL (newpage.html), meaning that the protocol and domain name pieces have been left out of the value of the href attribute.

```
14              <a href="newpage.html">This is a relative
            link to a new page.</a>
15          </p>
16          <p>
```
> This is also a relative link, but this link uses an image as the clickable piece of the link as opposed to text, as lines 8 and 7 do.

```
17              <a href="newpage.html"><img src="button.gif"
            alt="This image is a clickable button.">
            </a>
18          </p>
19          <p>
20              <a href="mailto:cheryl@chughes.com">This is
            link that launches an email message.</a>
21          </p>
22      </body>
23  </html>
```
> This link actually launches the default email program and creates a blank email message addressed to the email address referenced in the value of the href attribute. The special prefix mailto: keyword tells the Web browser that this link should create an email message. Clicking it will launch the default email program so the user can create a new email message to the recipient address listed in the link (cheryl@chughes.com).

Figure 2.15 Links Using the <a> Element

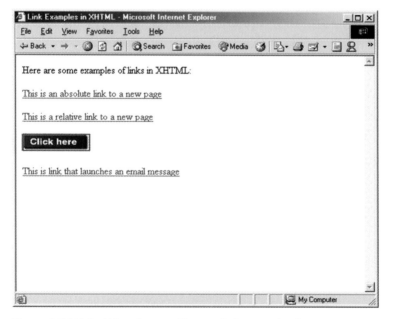

Figure 2.16 Links Using the <a> Element in Internet Explorer

Relative vs. Absolute URLs

Relative URLs are used to link documents that reside on the same Web server. When a relative URL is used, the protocol and domain name are omitted. The link to the target resource is relative to the location of the document containing the link, or the **source document**. If the target resource resides in the same directory as the source document, you can use a link containing only the name of the target resource, as in the first example below. If the target resource resides in a different directory on the Web server, you must include the subdirectory information in the link, as in the second two examples below. Here are some examples of using relative URLs in links:

☆ `<a href="newpage.html">Click Here</a>`

☆ `<a href="documents/newpage.html">Click Here</a>`

☆ `<a href="images/mypicture.gif">Click Here</a>`

Absolute URLs are used to link documents that reside on different Web servers. When an absolute URL is used, the protocol (`http://`) and domain name (`chughes.com`) are included to direct the Web browser to the location of the new Web server. The absolute URL does not take into account any location information about the current document and can reference any target resource anywhere on the Internet. Here are some examples of using absolute URLs in links:

☆ `<a href="http://chughes.com/newpage.html">Click Here</a>`

☆ `<a href="http://chughes.com/documents/newpage.html">Click Here</a>`

☆ `<a href="http://chughes.com/images/mypicture.gif">Click Here</a>`

Linking Within a Single Document

If you are working with a large document, you may want to create links to sections within that document. For example, you may want to create a link at the bottom of the document that links back to the top of the document, or a link that will take you to a footnote at the bottom of the page from within the body of the document. In order to create an **internal link**, you will need to first create the anchor at the place where you want the link to link to. The anchor element is used with an attribute called **name**, which identifies the anchor, or **target**:

```
<a name="footnote">Footnote</a>
```

Next, you need to create a link that looks like the relative links above, but has a # mark in front of the relative URL to tell the browser that this link exists in the current document. Following is an example:

```
<a href="#footnote">Link to footnote</a>
```

This would create an anchor where the footnote resides in the document, and clicking on the link would then take the user to that place within the document.

☆ Summary

▷ The three parts of an XHTML document are the document prolog, the header, and the body.

▷ The document framework elements encompass the body of the document and provide information about the document to programs.

▷ Block-level elements describe sections of content, while character-level elements describe words and phrases.

▷ The <font> element changes the look and color of text.

▷ XHTML has three sets of list elements: ordered, unordered, and definition.

☆ Online References

Reference Web site for all XHTML elements
`http://webdesign.about.com/library/tags/bl_index.htm`

W3C School's XHTML 1.0 element reference
`http://www.w3schools.com/xhtml/xhtml_reference.asp`

Introduction to XHTML with examples
`http://www.wdvl.com/Authoring/Languages/XML/XHTML/`

Character entity set: HTML+
`http://www.w3.org/MarkUp/HTMLPlus/htmlplus_13.html`

HTML ASCII reference
`http://www.w3schools.com/html/html_asciiref.asp`

☆ Review Questions

1. What are the three parts of an XHTML document?
2. What element must be present inside the <head> element?
3. What two elements must be present inside the <html> element?
4. Describe the purpose of a namespace.
5. What is the difference between the <br /> and <p> elements?
6. What is the difference between presentational and logical formatting elements?
7. What are the three types of lists and what is the difference between them?
8. Which <a> element attribute references the target document?
9. How would you use an anchor link to link back to the top of a long document?

☆ Hands-On Exercises

1. Create an XHTML document from the following HTML document. View your document in a browser and validate it on the W3C Markup Validation Web site.

```
<HTML>
<HEAD><TITLE>Exercise 1</TITLE></HEAD>
<BODY bgcolor="white">
<P>Popular Pets<BR>
<UL>
    <LI>Dog
    <LI>Cat
    <LI>Iguana
</UL>
</BODY>
</HTML>
```

2. Create the XHTML document from Figure 2.15 with links, view the page in a browser, and call it linktest.html.

3. Create the XHTML document from Figure 2.4. Use the `<div>` element to separate the sections of the document: the paragraph examples, the horizontal rule example, and the heading examples.

4. Find the character entities for the following symbols and create an XHTML document to test your results in a browser. Symbols: &, ~, {, }, and @

5. Create the following lists in XHTML, test your results in a browser, and validate the code at the W3C Markup Validation Web site.

Weekly Planner
   1 Monday
      • Pick up dry cleaning
      • Take dog to the vet
   2 Tuesday
   3 Wednesday
      • Change oil in car
      • Lunch with Wendy
      • Meeting with accountant
   4 Thursday
      • Go to grocery store
      • Pay phone bill
   5 Friday
      • Dinner and movie
   6 Saturday
   7 Sunday
      • Football game

Robin Williams Movies
   • Mrs. Doubtfire
   • Peter Pan
   • One Hour Photo

CHAPTER THREE

ADDING CASCADING STYLE SHEETS TO XHTML DOCUMENTS

This chapter covers the use of Cascading Style Sheets (CSS) to provide formatting for XHTML documents. By the end of this chapter you will understand how style sheets work in conjunction with XHTML documents to provide formatting information. You will also learn how to format CSS documents and use their rules and properties.

Chapter Objectives

☆ Learn how to use style sheets with XHTML documents

☆ Understand the syntax of Cascading Style Sheets

☆ Describe the properties and rules of Cascading Style Sheets

☆ Learn how to use the `class` and `id` attributes with style sheets

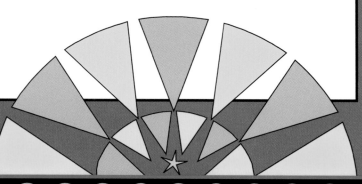

◎◎ Cascading Style Sheets

In 1996 the W3C recommended the adoption of a standard set of style sheets, **Cascading Style Sheets** Level 1 (CSS1). The original purpose of CSS was to provide HTML authors with more formatting support and give them a way to apply uniform styles to multiple documents. Cascading Style Sheets Level 2 (CSS2), introduced in 1998, included additional features and functionality.

CSS work with XHTML the same way they work with HTML, so if you are familiar with using them with HTML documents, you should find using them with XHTML easy. Because the CSS1 specification has been around for many years, Web browser support is widespread. Netscape Navigator 4.5 and above, and Internet Explorer 3.0 and above all support CSS.

Why Use Style Sheets?

So far, you have learned about a number of XHTML elements that can be used to lay out and format Web pages. So why would anyone want to use style sheets? The answer is that using style sheets allows you to separate a document's content from its presentation style and provides much greater control over document format.

Keeping the content and presentation information separate also allows you to change your presentation layout or method without having to modify the documents themselves, and allows you to apply one style sheet to any number of documents. For example, a winery that receives wine price data in an XHTML document could develop one style sheet that contained the formatting information for hundreds of documents. Or the winery could create multiple style sheets for presenting this data to customers: one for customers who request prices via a Web browser, another one for customers who request prices using a wireless Palm Pilot, and another for customers who call an automated phone line.

☆**TIP** **Separating Content from Presentation**

Web development is heading toward this idea of separating content from presentation. The XML family of technologies already clearly defines the boundaries between content and presentation. As you've noticed so far in this book, XHTML Strict does not provide support for many of the strictly presentational elements, such as HTML's `<font>` element.

The strictly presentational elements that are a part of the XHTML Transitional and XHTML Frameset versions of XHTML 1.0, including the `<font>` element, are primarily included for backward compatibility with existing HTML content. Because XHTML Strict does not include many of these presentation elements in its element set, it relies on style sheets to define presentational styles. XHTML Strict most closely represents the direction XHTML is heading. The W3C recommends that new content development should center around XHTML Strict whenever possible in order to be most compatible with future technologies.

◎◎ CSS Syntax

CSS contain rules and declarations that instruct a program, such as a Web browser, how to display certain elements. There are many styles that can be applied to XHTML documents. The CSS specification is extremely large, so we cover only a subset of its styles and declarations here. Links to more information and examples are provided at the end of the chapter.

Defining Styles

In order to use a style sheet with your XHTML document, you need to tell your document where to locate the style definitions. There are three ways to define styles:

1. *Linked Style Sheets* Style definitions in **linked style sheets** are stored in a file separate from the XHTML document. Linked style sheets provide style definitions to many documents—each document simply has to reference a single style sheet. Following is the syntax of the style sheet declaration in an XHTML document:

```
<link rel="stylesheet" href="mystyles.css" type="text/css" />
```

The <link> element is used to define the style sheet. The <link> element is an empty element and must be contained within the <head> element of an XHTML document. The rel attribute specifies this <link> element to be a link to a style sheet. The href attribute, like that for the <a> element, specifies the location of the style sheet file on the system. Both relative and absolute URLs can be used as the value for the href attribute. The type attribute declares this style sheet to be a plain-text file containing CSS styles.

2. *Global Style Sheets* **Global style sheets** are defined in the XHTML document, within the <style> element, which is contained within the <head> element. Following is the syntax of a global style sheet:

```
<head>
<title> Title of Document </title>
<style type="text/css">
<!--
p {
    color: red;
    font-family: arial
  }
-->
</style>
</head>
```

The <style> opening tag, like the <link> opening tag, defines the type of the style sheet to be plain-text CSS.

☆**WARNING**   **Defining Styles within XHTML Comments**

Notice that the section where the global styles are defined is contained within an XHTML comment. This is to hide the actual contents of the style definitions from older browsers that don't support CSS. The comment tags are not necessary to make CSS work, but if they are not provided in an XHTML document, older browsers may actually display the style property definitions on the Web page.

CSS Syntax

3. *Inline Styles* **Inline styles** are applied to a single element within the start tag of the element. If we wanted to assign certain properties to the text within a paragraph, we would include style definitions like the following:

```
<p style="color:red; font-family:arial">Paragraph text</p>
```

Style Precedence

An XHTML document can get its style information from any of these three methods or from a combination of any or all of them. When a style is defined in more than one place for a particular element the definition that is closest to the element itself is used.

For example, suppose that an XHTML document references a linked CSS file that defines style properties for the <h1> element, setting its font color to blue. The document then defines a global property within its <style> element that sets the font color for <h1> to red. Finally, a particular <h1> element within the document defines its font color to be purple by using the style attribute. Which style will be displayed in the browser? Will the content of the <h1> element be blue, red, or purple? The answer is purple. Inline styles on particular elements override global styles defined in the <style> element or in linked CSS files. In turn, global styles defined in the <style> element of an XHTML document override style settings from linked CSS files.

The ability to override styles gives developers a lot of power. For example, a developer could use a linked CSS file for the common formatting properties for all of the documents on a Web site. If one particular document needed special formatting properties, the developer could define global styles within that document without affecting the rest of the documents. The same is true for individual elements. A developer who wanted all of the <h1> elements in a document to be blue would define this in the <style> element or in a linked CSS file. If one particular <h1> element needed red text, the developer could define the red style on that particular element, which would override the blue setting of the other <h1> elements.

CSS Properties

There are many types of CSS properties:

1. **Font properties** define font styles such as font family or type, size, weight, and variant.

2. **Text properties** define the layout of blocks of text, words, or characters, including spacing, alignment, transformation (forced uppercase or lowercase), and decoration (such as underline, overline, strikethrough, and blinking).

3. **Color and image properties** define the color and background formatting of text and images. These properties can also define the position of a background image and whether the image is repeated (tiled).

4. **Border properties** define the style of borders for elements like tables and images, as well as for the entire document. Border properties include width, height, style, color, margins, and padding.

5. **Display properties** define styles for the structure of the document. These properties can define the placement of elements within the document, such as block or inline, and how whitespace is formatted within the document.

Appendix B defines some of the properties most often used for each of these categories. Again, because the CSS specification is very large, only a subset of the available properties is defined in this chapter and in the appendix.

CSS Rules

CSS rules have two parts: a **selector** and a set of **property declarations** that define the style or styles that will apply to the selector. The selector can contain a single element, a class/id selector, or a list of selectors. Multiple selectors are separated by commas. For styles that have more than one property defined, each property is separated by a semicolon. Following is an example of a rule that applies to the <h1> element:

```
h1 {
        color:   black;
        font-size:   12pt;
        font-family:   arial
     }
```

The following rule applies to three elements, <h1>, <h2> and <p>:

```
h1, h2, p   {
        color:   red;
        font-size:   12pt;
        font-family:   arial
     }
```

☆ SHORTCUT   **Single Property Rules**

When a rule assigns only one property, no semicolon is needed after the property definition:
```
h1   {
        font-size:   12pt
     }
```

CSS Comments

The syntax for comments in CSS is different than we've seen so far for XHTML documents. Following is an example of a comment in CSS:

```
/*   This is a comment   */
/*   Comments can also
       span multiple lines */
```

Comments begin with /*, followed by the content of the comment, and end with */. They can span multiple lines. Web browsers and other processing applications ignore comments in CSS files.

Classes and IDs

You may be wondering what to do if you need to assign more than one style to the same element. For example, suppose you define the following style for the `<p>` element:

```
p   {
        color: red
    }
```

If you define the `<p>` element like this, all paragraphs in your document will be formatted with red text. What if you need some of the paragraphs to be formatted with red text and others to be formatted with black text? The answer is to use a **class** or **id selector**.

Class and id selectors are used to define styles that are independent of elements. Classes can be used to define styles for any number of elements and for any number of occurrences of elements in a document. The `id` attribute occurs only once in a document, so it should not be used to declare styles for a number of elements. For example, if you know that a certain element in a document will be used to uniquely identify the document, but you are not sure which element it will be in each document, you can use the `id` selector to generically reference the unique element independent of the document itself. We look at an example of this a little later in the chapter.

Each of these styles can be defined in the XHTML document by using the `class` and `id` attributes. Following are examples of each:

Class selector:

Style sheet: `.class_example {`
```
                            color: red
                        }
```
XHTML document reference: `<p class="class_example">`

ID selector:

Style sheet: `#id_example    {`
```
                            color: black
                        }
```
XHTML document reference: `<p id="id_example">`

Using `class` and `id` selectors for style formatting requires certain changes to the XHTML document because the appropriate attributes must be defined for each element to be formatted.

Classes can also be assigned to individual elements to allow more control over formatting. This is done by placing the name of an element in front of the period in a class style declaration. For example, the following defines class formatting styles that apply only to the `<p>` element:

```
p              {
                   color: black
               }
p.red_text     {
                   color: red
               }
p.cyan_text    {
                   color: cyan
               }
```

These declarations set font colors for the <p> element depending on which class is defined in the element. If no `class` attribute is specified, then the declaration for the <p> element of black is applied.

Link Rules

CSS provides special declarations to define specific events as opposed to elements. For example, the anchor element, <a>, is used to define links in a document. As you may have noticed while surfing the Web, links to pages are usually blue. Once you click on a specific link, that link changes color, usually to purple, in order to show that the page has been visited. This way, when you come back to a page, the links you have already visited are purple and the links you have not yet visited are still blue.

CSS provides special properties to control these colors. They are designated by the element name followed by a colon and then the property name. There are four of these classes defined in CSS1:

1. *Link* is used for links that have not yet been visited.

2. *Visited* is used for links that have been visited.

3. *Active* is used when the user clicks on the link.

4. *Hover* is used when the user places the mouse cursor over a link.

The following shows how to define these properties in a style sheet:

```
a:link         {
                   color: blue
               }
a:visited      {
                   color: purple
               }
a:active       {
                   color: red
               }
a:hover        {
                   color: yellow
               }
```

In this example, all unvisited links in the document will be blue and visited links will be purple. When a user moves the mouse over any link on the page the link will turn yellow, and when the user clicks on the link it will turn red.

◎◎ Style Sheets in Action

Now that you are familiar with the syntax of CSS and where to declare styles and style sheets, let's look at a couple of examples. Figure 3.1 is our course description XHTML document with a linked CSS file defined on line 7:

```
1   <?xml version="1.0"?>
2   <!DOCTYPE html PUBLIC "-//W3C//DTD XHTML 1.0 Strict//EN"
3       "http://www.w3.org/TR/xhtml1/DTD/xhtml1-strict.dtd">
4   <html xmlns="http://www.w3.org/1999/xhtml">
5       <head>                                    Style sheet declaration
6           <title>Introduction to XHTML</title>
7           <link rel="stylesheet" href="mystyles.css" type="text/css" />
8       </head>
9       <body>
10          <strong>Course Name:</strong>  Introduction to XHTML <br />
11          <strong>Course Number: </strong>  CS 112 <br />
12          <strong>Instructor: </strong> T. Perdue <br />
13          <strong>Meeting Time: </strong>  Wednesday,
            5:30pm - 7:30pm <br />
14          <p>
15          <strong>Course Description: </strong> This course covers the
16          basics of how to write XHTML Web documents.
17          </p>
18          <strong>Prerequisites: </strong>
19          <ul>
20              <li>CS 101 - Introduction to Computers </li>
21              <li>CS 103 - Introduction to Web Site Design </li>
22              <li>CS 110 - Designing Web Pages with HTML </li>
23          </ul>
24      </body>
25  </html>
```

Figure 3.1 XHTML Document course-descriptions.html with Linked Style Sheet

Notice that the <link> element is nested within the <head> element. Figure 3.2 is the style sheet, mystyles.css, for this XML document.

Figures 3.3 and 3.4 show what this XHTML document looks like with and without the style sheet properties applied to the elements.

```
1    strong {
2                  font-weight:bold;
3                  text-align:left;
4                  background-color:yellow;
5                  text-decoration:underline
6          }
7    li    {
8                  font-style:italic;
9                  color:purple
10         }
```

Figure 3.2 CSS mystyles.css

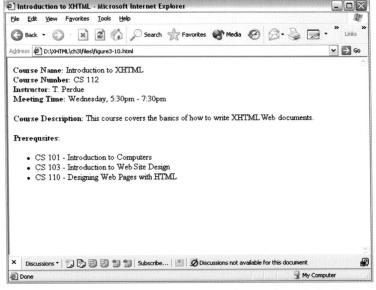

Figure 3.3 XHTML Document in Internet Explorer without Style Sheet

☆ **SHORTCUT**   **Do This Exercise Yourself**

To do this exercise yourself, use a text editor to create two files: the XHTML file course-description.html and the CSS mystyles.css. Save both files into the same directory on your hard drive. Then open the XHTML file in Internet Explorer, and you should see your formatted document. To see the document without the formatting, just remove the reference to the style sheet on line 7 of the XHTML document.

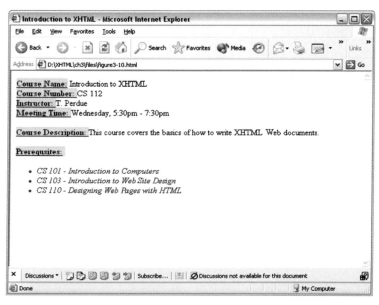

Figure 3.4 XHTML Document in Internet Explorer with Style Sheet mystyles.css

Figure 3.5 shows the same document with the styles defined inside the XHTML document. The two documents will display exactly the same when viewed in a browser.

```
1    <?xml version="1.0"?>
2    <!DOCTYPE html PUBLIC "-//W3C//DTD XHTML 1.0 Strict//EN"
3        "http://www.w3.org/TR/xhtml1/DTD/xhtml1-strict.dtd">
4    <html xmlns="http://www.w3.org/1999/xhtml">
5        <head>
6            <title>Introduction to XHTML</title>
7            <style type="text/css">
8                <!--
9                strong    {
10                               font-weight:bold;
11                               text-align:left;
12                               background-color:yellow;
13                               text-decoration:underline
14                           }
15               li         {
16                               font-style:italic;
17                               color:purple
18                           }
19                -->
20          </style>
```

Figure 3.5 XHTML Document course-descriptions_2.html with Global Style Sheet (*continues*)

Style Sheets in Action

```
21    </head>
22    <body>
23       <strong>Course Name:</strong>  Introduction to XHTML <br />
24       <strong>Course Number: </strong>  CS 112 <br />
25       <strong>Instructor: </strong> T. Perdue <br />
26       <strong>Meeting Time: </strong> Wednesday, 5:30pm-7:30pm <br />
27       <p>
28       <strong>Course Description: </strong> This course covers
29       the basics of how to write XHTML Web documents.
30       </p>
31       <strong>Prerequisites: </strong>
32       <ul>
33          <li>CS 101 - Introduction to Computers </li>
34          <li>CS 103 - Introduction to Web Site Design </li>
35          <li>CS 110 - Designing Web Pages with HTML </li>
36       </ul>
37    </body>
38 </html>
```

Figure 3.5 XHTML Document course-descriptions_2.html with Global Style Sheet (*continued*)

Using Universal Values

If you would like to apply rules to all of the elements in a document, unless an element explicitly overrides the rule, you can use the special declaration "*."

```
1    strong   {
2                     font-weight:bold;
3                     text-align:left;
4                     background-color:yellow;
5                     text-decoration:underline
6              }
7    li       {
8                     font-style:italic;
9                     color:purple
10             }
11   *         {
12                    color:green
13             }
```

Figure 3.6 CSS mystyles2.css

Figure 3.6 adds a default style to our style sheet from Figure 3.2. In Figure 3.6, lines 11 through 13 declare the default font color to be green. Unless an element overrides this setting, its font color will be green. The element <li> explicitly defines the color and font, which overrides the green font setting from the default element.

Let's apply this style sheet to our XHTML document. Figure 3.7 shows the document in a browser. You'll notice now that all of the text, except for the text in the `<li>` elements, is now green. Green will be the default font color for all text in the document unless an element overrides this setting with its own property definition.

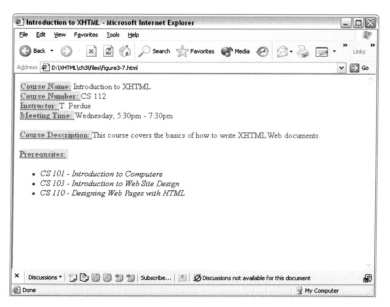

Figure 3.7 XHTML Document in Internet Explorer with Style Sheet mystlyes2.css

☆**TIP   Don't Forget to Rename the Style Sheet**

If you want to try this example for yourself, don't forget to change the name of the style sheet file in your XHTML document in the `<link>` element to mystyles2.css.

Property Inheritance

You learned about element nesting in Chapter 2. Elements that are contained within other elements are said to be **children** of the outer elements, and the outer elements are referred to as **parents** of the nested elements. This hierarchy of elements is applied to CSS in the form of **property inheritance**. Property inheritance means that properties defined for parent elements are passed along to child elements, unless the child element overrides it. For example, if the parent of an element sets its font to 18 points, the child elements will also have a font size of 18 points unless they declare their own rules to override the rules defined by the parent.

Using the same XHTML document, let's define a new style sheet:

```
1    body    {
2                  color:green;
3                  font-style:normal;
4                  font-size:12
5            }
6    strong  {
7                  color:white;
8                  background-color:blue
9            }
10   p       {
11                 margin-top:50px;
12                 color:blue;
13                 background-color:yellow;
14                 font-size:20pt;
15                 font-style:italic;
16                 border-style:double
17           }
```

Figure 3.8 CSS mystyles3.css

In Figure 3.8, lines 2 through 4 are the property rules for the <body> element. These rules will be applied to all of the child elements of <body> unless they are overridden by the child element. Lines 7 and 8 define property rules for the <strong> element, and lines 11 through 16 define rules for the <p> element that override the rules set in the parent element, <body>. Figure 3.9 shows the XHTML document in a browser.

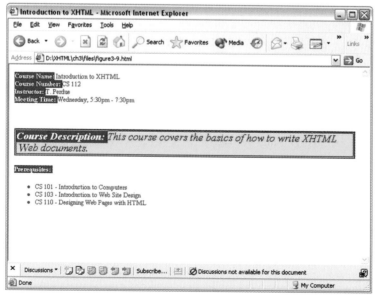

Figure 3.9 XHTML Document in Internet Explorer with Style Sheet mystyles3.css

Notice that the text of all content within the <strong> elements is white, which overrides the settings of the <strong> element's parent, <body>, which sets the font color to green. Also notice that the course description text on lines 15 and 16 of the XHTML code in Figure 3.10 is contained within the <p> element, so the style settings for the <p> element as defined in the style sheet will override the settings for <body>. And, within the <p> tags on lines 14 and 17 of the XHTML document in Figure 3.10, the <strong> element with the text "Course Description" is defined by the <strong> element's style definitions, not the <p> or the <body> element.

Using Class and ID Selectors

Let's look at a more complex example that uses the class and id attributes. For this example, we'll define a linked along with a global style sheet. We'll also include a few inline styles as well. Figure 3.10 shows the linked style sheet that we'll use for this example, mystyles4.css. Figure 3.11 shows our XHTML document, and Figure 3.12 shows how the document looks in a browser.

```
1   /*  Defines a class called underline */
2   div.box {
3           margin-top:50px;
4           background-color:yellow;
5           color:#000090;
6           border-style:double;
7           padding: 10px;
8           border-color: #000090
9           }
10
11  /*  Defines styles for the <p> element */
12  p   {
13          font-size:16pt
14      }
15
16  /* Defines specific properties for the <p> element with
17  the class name of description */
18  p.description {
19              color: #000099;
20              background-color:#cccccc;
21              font-style:italic;
22              }
23
24   /* Defines a unique id selector that will be applied
25      to one element within the document */
26   #identifier   {
27              color: red
28              }
26
27   /* Defines class to align text to the right */
```

Figure 3.10 CSS mystyles4.css (*continues*)

```
28
29  .right {
30     text-align: right
31     }
32
33  /* Defines universal element formatting styles */
34  * {
35     color:   #333333;
36     font-family: arial;
37     font-size: 10pt
38     }
```

Figure 3.10 CSS mystyles4.css (*continued*)

```
1   <?xml version="1.0"?>
2   <!DOCTYPE html PUBLIC "-//W3C//DTD XHTML 1.0 Strict//EN"
3       "http://www.w3.org/TR/xhtml1/DTD/xhtml1-strict.dtd">
4   <html xmlns="http://www.w3.org/1999/xhtml">
5     <head>
6        <title>Introduction to XHTML</title>
7        <link rel="stylesheet" href="mystyles4.css"
              type="text/css" />
8        <style type="text/css">
9           <!--
10          h1 {
11              font-size: 20;
12              text-align:center;
13              font-style:italic;
14              }
15          h2 {
16              font-size: 18;
17              text-align:left;
18              font-style:italic;
19              }
20          h3 {
21              font-size: 16;
22              text-align:left;
23              font-style:italic;
24              }
25          -->
26       </style>
27     </head>
28     <body>
29        <h1> Course Description   </h1>
30        <div class="box">
31           <div class="right"><strong>Course Name:
                 </strong>Introduction to XHTML <br /></div>
```

Figure 3.11 XHTML Document with Linked and Global Style Sheets and Inline Styles
(*continues*)

```
32              <strong>Course Number: </strong> CS 112 <br />
33              <strong>Instructor: </strong> T. Perdue <br />
34              <strong>Meeting Time: </strong>
35                  Wednesday, 5:30pm - 7:30pm <br />
36          </div>
37          <h2 id="identifier">Course Description: </h2>
38          <p class="description">This course covers the
                basics of how to write XHTML Web documents.
39          </p>
40          <h3>Prerequisites: </h3>
41          <ul>
42              <li>CS 101 - Introduction to Computers </li>
43              <li>CS 103 - Introduction to Web Site Design </li>
44              <li>CS 110 - Designing Web Pages with HTML </li>
45          </ul>
46      </body>
47 </html>
```

Figure 3.11 XHTML Document with Linked and Global Style Sheets and Inline Styles
(*continued*)

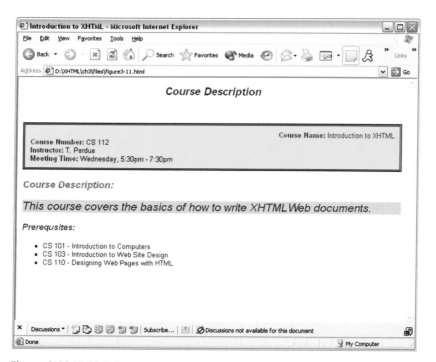

Figure 3.12 XHTML Document in Browser

Validating Style Sheets

The W3C provides a tool on its Web site that will validate CSS documents, much like the XHTML validator that we used earlier in the book. Figure 3.13 shows the W3C CSS-validating Web site.

Figure 3.13 The W3C CSS Validator Web Site

☆ Summary

▷ Style sheets contain structure rules that allow you to determine the format and presentation of XHTML documents.

▷ CSS uses property rules to define various presentation styles and settings, including those for font, text, border, display, and color.

▷ Child elements can inherit CSS properties from parent elements.

▷ CSS style definitions can reside either inside the XHTML document or as an external file.

▷ `Class` and `id` selectors are used to define element-independent styles.

▷ Universal values can be defined as formatting styles for the entire document using the "`*`" character.

☆ Online References

W3C CSS Specification
`http://www.w3.org/Style/CSS`

Web Review Style Sheet Reference Guide and Browser Support
`http://www.webreview.com/style/css1/charts/mastergrid.shtml`

Webmonkey Style Sheet Guide
`http://hotwired.lycos.com/webmonkey/reference/stylesheet_guide/`

CSS property and syntax
`http://www.blooberry.com/indexdot/css/`

W3C CSS Validator
`http://jigsaw.w3.org/css-validator/`

☆ Review Questions

1. How can CSS be used to provide style information to many documents?

2. What does *precedence* mean and how does it affect styles defined in linked files as opposed to global styles in an XHTML document?

3. What is a *style property* and how is it used to define a particular formatting style for an element?

4. What is the difference between the `class` and `id` selectors?

5. What declaration would you use if you wanted all of the text to be in the Arial typeface?

6. What property would you define if you wanted to set the color of all visited links to red?

7. Define property inheritance and how it can be used to format elements.

☆ Hands-On Exercises

1. Write the style sheet declaration statement for a style sheet at the following location:

   `http://www.chughes.com/styles.css`

2. Create the property rules for an element called <h1> that has the following formatting styles: font size of 12 points, bold style, blue text color.

3. Define a style sheet that sets links to the colors below. For all of the links, turn off the underlining. Create the XHTML document with a global style sheet and test it in a browser.

   ```
   Unvisited link:   green
   Visited link:     purple
   Active:    red
   Hover:     blue
   ```

4. Create an external style sheet called ex-4.css for the following XHTML document that will produce the output shown below. Do not use default properties; instead, define styles for each element in its own set of properties. You may have to change the XHTML code. Validate your CSS document on the W3C Web site using the validator.

   ```
   1   <?xml version="1.0"?>
   2   <!DOCTYPE html PUBLIC "-//W3C//DTD XHTML 1.0 Strict//EN"
   3       "http://www.w3.org/TR/xhtml1/DTD/xhtml1-strict.dtd">
   4   <html xmlns="http://www.w3.org/1999/xhtml">
   5      <head>
   6         <title>Introduction to XHTML</title>
   7         <link rel="stylesheet" href="ex-4.css"
           type="text/css" />
   8      </head>
   9      <body>
   10        <h1>XHTML Users Club</h1>
   11        <p>9 Pond Ave.</p>
   12        <p>Boston</p>
   13        <p>MA</p>
   14        <p>02109</p>
   15        <h2>617-555-1234</h2>
   16     </body>
   17  </html>
   ```

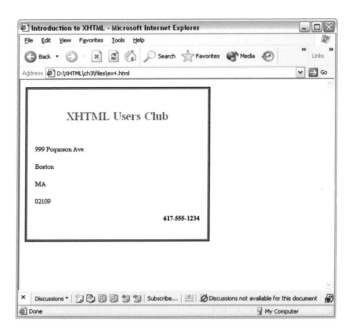

5. Use the XHTML document from Exercise 4 to create a document that contains the style properties from ex-4.css within the `<style>` element of the document.

CHAPTER FOUR

BRINGING WEB PAGES TO LIFE WITH IMAGES AND MULTIMEDIA

T his chapter explains how to include images in XHTML documents. You will learn about Web-friendly image formats and how to use XHTML elements to include graphics in XHTML documents. You will also learn how to create images that are links to other documents and how to create image maps.

◎◎ Chapter Objectives

☆ Learn how to include images and pictures in Web pages

☆ Understand how to use images as links

☆ Learn how to create image maps

☆ Describe how to include multimedia, such as audio and video, on Web pages

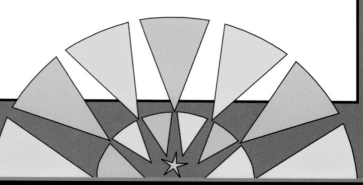

◎◉ Images and Multimedia on the Web

One of the features of the Web that has made it so popular compared to other Internet technologies like telnet and gopher is the ability to include images on Web pages. Without images, the Web would be far less exciting to browse through! As Web technologies continue to advance, and as the surfing population gains broader access to high-speed Internet connections, the quality and quantity of image- and multimedia-related content on the Web have skyrocketed. Many types of multimedia content, such as audio and video files, can now be incorporated into Web pages.

◎◉ Inline Images and the `<img>` Element

Let's start with the image element, `<img>`. The `<img>` is an empty element. It is actually considered to be a linking element, much like the `<a>` element. Although many HTML programmers do not think of the `<img>` element as a linking element, it is, in fact, used to embed images into an HTML page. The `<img>` element, unlike the `<a>` element, does not require any user intervention, such as clicking on highlighted text, in order to activate the link. Following is the syntax of an `<img>` element:

```
<img src="myimage.gif" alt="Alternate text for my image" />
```

Image File Formats

Web browsers can link to any type of image format. The problem is that browsers have built-in support for only a few image file types. If you save your image files in one of the standard formats, you can be assured that most Web surfers will be able to see your images. In this section, we cover the file formats that most browsers support. Later in this chapter, we discuss multimedia formats.

GIF and JPEG

The **Graphics Interchange Format** (GIF) and **Joint Photographic Experts Group** (JPEG) format have been in use on the Web for many years. Every graphical Web browser developed since the early 1990s supports these two image formats. Most image-editing programs have options to save images in one of these two formats, so you should have no problems creating Web images from other image formats.

GIF was created by CompuServe as a cross-platform image format. GIF images are usually very small, so they load quickly into browsers and are easy to store since they take up very little space. GIF only supports 256 colors, so this format is best for nonphotographic images, like buttons, bullets, and separator lines. Because of the limited number of colors, high-quality images like photographs seem grainy. The JPEG format is the better choice for high-quality images.

The JPEG format was developed by the Joint Photographic Experts Group for storing high-quality images like photographs. Typically, photographic image files are extremely large, and even a small number of them could very quickly fill up your hard drive. The JPEG format technically isn't a format but rather a compression technique that can be used by other image formats to reduce the file size. Depending on the graphic editing program being used, there may be several JPEG options with various levels of compression.

There is always a trade-off between size of the file and quality. For example, a popular high-quality image format used by many graphic designers is the **tagged image format** (TIF). TIF allows users to store image files in an extremely high-quality format. However, TIF files are very large, which doesn't translate well for the Web because large files take a long time to download over a dial-up connection. A TIF file that is saved as a JPEG file, however, is much smaller yet retains much of the image quality.

PNG

The **Portable Network Graphics** (PNG) format was originally introduced as a replacement technology for GIF by the W3C. The recommendation was released in 1996. According to the W3C, PNG is

> an extensible file format for the lossless, portable, well-compressed storage of raster images. PNG provides a patent-free replacement for GIF and can also replace many common uses of Tagged Image File Format TIFF. Indexed-color, grayscale, and true color images are supported, plus an optional alpha channel for transparency.

It is unlikely that PNG will replace JPEG because JPEG works well with high-quality images. One of the biggest advantages PNG has over GIF is that it is not limited to 256 colors. PNG files, like GIF files, are usually small. PNG didn't catch on like some expected it to, so although most new browsers offer support for this image format, JPEG and GIF are still the most popular formats on the Web.

The <img> Element Attributes

The <img> element has two required attributes, src and alt. The value of the src (source) attribute, like the href attribute, is the URL of the target resource—the image file in this case. The value can be an absolute or relative URL. The value of the alt (alternate text) attribute contains a text string that will display in the place of the image file if the client program cannot display images, or when the mouse moves over the image in some browsers.

When a browser that is reading an XHTML page encounters an <img> element, it automatically sends an additional request to the Web server asking for the image file referenced in the src attribute. After the image file is returned to the Web browser, it displays the image file in the page exactly where the <img> element is located. These images are called **inline images**, because they are loaded into the browser window at the same time as the rest of the HTML document.

Let's look at an example. Figure 4.1 contains an XHTML file that displays an image file in a Web browser. Figure 4.2 shows the page in a graphical browser (Internet Explorer), and Figure 4.3 shows what this page looks like in the Lynx text-based browser.

☆**TIP**   **Always Include an `alt` Attribute**

It is very important to include the `alt` attribute with the `<img>` element. The text in the `alt` attribute will show up in place of the image on clients that cannot render graphics, such as most cell phones, handheld PDAs, and text-based browsers. This is especially important if you are using your images as links. The `alt` attribute is extremely important for the visually impaired user who relies on a speech-enabled browser. If the browser encounters an image it will read the value of the `alt` element to the user. It is one of the recommendations found in the Web Accessibility Initiative (WAI) sponsored by the W3C. The link to the WAI home page is listed at the end of this chapter if you would like more information.

If you do not want any text to show up for an image, set the `alt` attribute equal to an empty string: `alt=""`. For example, many Web developers use small, transparent (or invisible) image files to help them with page layouts. These images are never intended to be seen, either with a graphical or text browser. Setting the `alt` attribute to an empty string prevents it from showing up in nongraphical browsers.

```
1   <?xml version="1.0"?>
2   <!DOCTYPE html PUBLIC "-//W3C//DTD XHTML 1.0 Strict//EN"
3       "http://www.w3.org/TR/xhtml1/DTD/xhtml1-strict.dtd">
4   <html xmlns="http://www.w3.org/1999/xhtml">
5       <head>
6           <title>Sample Image</title>
7       </head>
8       <body>
9           <p>
10              This Web page contains our first image file:
11          </p>
12          <p>
13              <img src="myimage.gif" alt="Alternate text for my image" />
14          </p>
15          <p>
16              Isn't this fun?
17          </p>
18      </body>
19  </html>
```

> The image element. Notice that the text in the `alt` attribute shows up in place of the image file in the text browser: "Alternate text for my image."

Figure 4.1 XHTML Document with myimage.html

☆**WARNING**   **The `alt` Attribute Is Required in the XHTML DTD**

Be aware that creating an `<img>` element in XHTML without an `alt` attribute will cause an error if you test this page in a validator because the `alt` attribute is required for the `<img>` element according to the XHTML DTD. But, because the `alt` attribute was not a required attribute in HTML, most browsers will display the page fine.

Inline Images and the `<img>` Element

Figure 4.2 Image Document in Internet Explorer with myimage.html

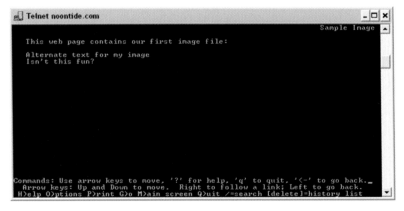

Figure 4.3 Image Document in Lynx Text Browser with myimage.html

Now, let's remove the `alt` attribute and see how it affects the way our page displays. In the XHTML code from Figure 4.1, change line 13 to

```
<img src="myimage.gif" />
```

Figure 4.4 shows the modified document in a browser, and Figure 4.5 shows the page in the Lynx text-based browser. Notice that in Internet Explorer, a graphical browser, the page has not changed, but in Lynx the page now has `[myimage.gif]` where the image should be instead of the alternate text from Figure 4.3. If no `alt` tag is specified, text browsers will simply display the name of the image file, which isn't very helpful.

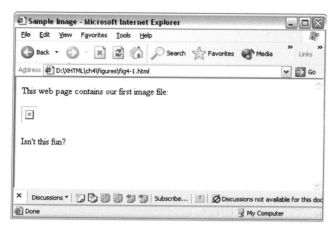

Figure 4.4 Image myimage-no-alt.html Document in Internet Explorer

Figure 4.5 Image myimage-no-alt.html Document in Lynx Text Browser

The <img> element has a number of other attributes for XHTML, as listed in Figure 4.6.

Using the <img> Element for Linking

Images on the Web are commonly used with the anchor element, <a>. If you embed an <img> element within an <a> element, the image becomes clickable, meaning clicking anywhere on the image activates the <a> element and the user is redirected to the page the <a> element references. Here is how you would create an image as a link:

```
<a href="newpage.html"><img src="myimage.gif" alt="Click on
this image" /></a>
```

Attribute Name	Description and Values
alt	Text description of the image used in place of the image on nongraphical browsers. *Value*: text string
height	Sets the height of the image. *Value*: pixels or percentage
ismap	Defines the images to be an image map that is processed on the server (server-side image map). *Value*: ismap
longdesc	Contains a URI that links to a document with a long description of the image. *Value*: URI
src	Contains a URL to the location of the image that is being referenced. *Value*: URL
usemap	Defines the images to be an image map that is processed on the client (client-side image map). *Value*: text string identifier
width	Sets the width of the image. *Value*: pixels or percentage

Figure 4.6 Attributes for `<img>` Element

Let's modify our XHTML file from Figure 4.1 to make the image file a link. Figure 4.7 shows the new XHTML file and Figure 4.8 shows how the page looks in a browser.

Notice that the image in Figure 4.8 now has a blue box around it. Web browsers automatically place a blue box around images that are being used as links to identify them as clickable objects. You can turn this off by using the border style sheet property. Adding the following style sheet declaration to the document in Figure 4.7 will turn off the blue border around the image:

```
<style type="text/css">
   img { border: none; }
</style>
```

```
1   <?xml version="1.0"?>
2   <!DOCTYPE html PUBLIC "-//W3C//DTD XHTML 1.0 Strict//EN"
3       "http://www.w3.org/TR/xhtml1/DTD/xhtml1-strict.dtd">
4   <html xmlns="http://www.w3.org/1999/xhtml">
5       <head>
6           <title>Sample Image as a Link</title>
7       </head>
8       <body>
9           <p>
10              This Web page contains a linked image file:
11          </p>
12          <p>
13              <a href="newpage.html"><img src="myimage.gif"
                    alt="Click here" /></a>
14          </p>
15          <p>
16              Isn't this fun?
17          </p>
18      </body>
19  </html>
```

Figure 4.7 XHTML myimagelink.html Document

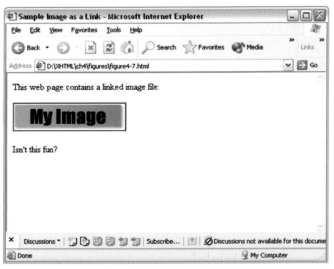

Figure 4.8 Image myimagelink.html Document in Internet Explorer

◎◎ Creating Image Maps

As you've seen, images can be used as linking elements when used in conjunction with the <a> element. Using them in this way makes the entire image a link to the page specified in the href attribute of the <a> element. You can click anywhere in the image and you will be directed to the page that the <a> element references. You can also make different parts of the image link to different places using **image maps**.

Image maps are a combination of images and XHTML code. Image maps need both an image file and a map in order to work. The map contains sets of pixel coordinates that define different shaped areas on the image.

☆WARNING   Image Maps Will Not Work in Most Nongraphical Browsers

Because image maps are designed to be graphical, they will not work in most nongraphical browsers. Some text-based Web browsers, like Lynx, will display a list of the links that are available in the map, but the graphical reference of the image map is lost. If you are creating content that you think may be accessed by nongraphical clients, you may want to stay away from image maps. If you do use them, be sure to use the alt tag for each of the links to provide a description of each of the links.

Client-side and Server-side Image Maps

Client-side and *server-side* refer to where the map file is located and which program is responsible for interpreting clicks to determine where to send the request. Server-side image maps store and execute the map file on the server, and client-side image maps store the map in the XHTML page and are executed on the client, or browser. Server-side image maps are obsolete for the most part, so we only cover client-side image maps in this section. See the TIP box for more information about server-side image maps.

☆TIP   Use Client-Side Image Maps

In the early days of the Web, server-side image maps were very common. Server-side image maps stored the map file on the server and the server was responsible for interpreting user clicks. This was because early versions of Web browsers did not know how to handle image maps. But this added overhead to the server and caused the browser to send a request back to the server every time a user clicked on the image map. Web browsers started incorporating client-side support for image maps around 1997, so there is really no reason to use server-side image maps anymore. The current standard for image maps is client-side. Following are a couple of links about server-side image maps:

http://www.wdvl.com/Authoring/HTML/Objects/Ssmap.html
http://hotwired.lycos.com/webmonkey/html/96/39/index2a.html

Creating Image Maps

To create a client-side image map, you will need to know the coordinates of the areas within your image that you would like to make into links. Figure 4.9 describes the shapes that can be used to define areas on an image map.

Shape	Pixel Coordinates	Description
circle, circ	x, y, r	The x and y designate the center of the circle, and the r represents the radius.
rectangle, rect	x1, y1, x2, y2	Designates the upper-left and lower-right corner coordinates of the rectangle.
polygon, poly	x1, y1, x2, y2, x3, y3, etc.	Designates a multisided polygon. Each corner of the polygon is represented by an x/y coordinate. The polygon must have at least three corners.
default	N/A	The default area encompasses all areas of the image that are not part of an area defined by the clickable shapes.

Figure 4.9 Shapes for Clickable Areas in Image Maps

Creating a Client-side Image Map

Let's create an image map using the image in Figure 4.10. We'll create three clickable areas, as shown in Figure 4.11: a circle on the red balloon, a rectangle on the blue balloon, and a polygon on the yellow balloon. Note that these shaded areas will not show up in a browser if you create an image map, they just show where the clickable areas are located for the purpose of this example. The image map is declared within the <img> start tag by the usemap attribute. This attribute contains the name of the image map to use for this image. These maps are defined within the <map> elements, which you will learn about below.

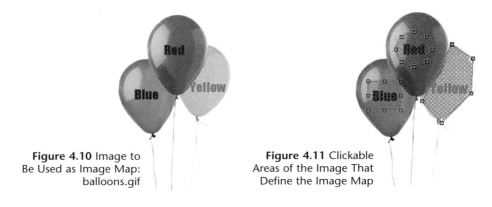

Figure 4.10 Image to Be Used as Image Map: balloons.gif

Figure 4.11 Clickable Areas of the Image That Define the Image Map

★ **TIP**   **Software for Creating Image Maps**

There are a number of freeware and shareware programs you can use to create the maps for your image maps, but you don't necessarily need to use any special programs to create them. You just need to know the coordinates as described in Figure 4.13 for each shape area. For this example, a shareware program called MapEdit is used. There are links at the end of this chapter to a few popular image map-editing programs. Note that some of these programs were developed for HTML, not XHTML, so you may need to manually change the code that the programs create to make them XHTML compliant.

The map itself is contained within the <map> element. The <map> element has only one required attribute, id, which is used to uniquely identify the image map within the document. The name attribute has been used in previous versions of HTML to identify the name of the image map, so it is good practice to add both the id and name attribute for now. The name attribute is included in all three versions of XHTML. The value of the name and id attributes should match the name given in the usemap attribute of the <img> element where the image for the map is located. Each of the clickable areas within the map is contained within an <area /> empty element. The <area /> element's attributes describe each of the areas. Following are the attributes for <area />:

1. shape defines which shape, as defined in Figure 4.9, this area will take.

2. cords defines the coordinates for the shape.

3. href or nohref describe the URL that clicking on this area will link to. Assigning the nohref attribute means that there is no link for this area. This attribute must be set equal to itself to remain XHTML compliant: nohref="nohref"

4. alt is for alternate text, like the <img> element.

The alt attribute is the only required attribute for the <area /> element. The XHTML document for our image map is shown in Figure 4.12.

```
1   <?xml version="1.0" ?>
2   <!DOCTYPE html PUBLIC "-//W3C//DTD XHTML 1.0 Strict//EN"
3       "http://www.w3.org/TR/xhtml1/DTD/xhtml1-strict.dtd">
4   <html xmlns="http://www.w3.org/1999/xhtml">
5       <head>
6           <title>Sample Image</title>
7           <style type="text/css">
8               img { border: none; }
9           </style>
10      </head>
11      <body>
12          <p>
13              This Web page contains our first image file:
14          </p>
15          <p>
16              <img src="balloons.gif" alt="Click on this image"
                    usemap="#myimage" />
17          </p>
18          <p>
19              Isn't this fun?
20              <map name="myimage" id="myimage">
21              <area shape="circle" alt="Red Balloon"
                    coords="155,123,34" href="red.html"
22                  title="Red Balloon" />
23              <area shape="rect" alt="Blue Balloon"
                    coords="68,185,130,242" href="blue.html"
24                  title="Blue Balloon" />
25              <area shape="poly" alt="Yellow Balloon"
26                  coords="227,114,227,114,227,113,171,224,
27                  208,267,264,209,264,209,267,141"
                    href="yellow.html" title="Yellow Balloon" />
28              <area shape="rect" alt="Default Area"
29                  href="default.html" coords="0,0,307,411" />
30          </map>
31          </p>
32      </body>
33  </html>
```

The usemap attribute is set to the name of the map and is designated as a link within this page by the beginning #sign.

Begins the image map with the opening <map> element. The name and id attribute values match the name given for this map on line 11.

Defines the circle area for the red balloon in our image. It sets the URL or the href attribute to red.html and sets the alternate text in the alt attribute to "Red Balloon."

Defines the rectangle area for the blue balloon in our image. It sets the URL for the href attribute to blue.html and sets the alternate text in the alt attribute to "Blue Balloon."

Defines the polygon area for the yellow balloon in our image. It sets the URL for the href attribute to yellow.html and sets the alternate text in the alt attribute to "Yellow Balloon." Notice the large number of coordinates in the coords attribute; this is due to the fact that this polygon has many sides.

Defines the default area that encompasses all areas of the image not contained within one of the other clickable areas. If users click outside the circle, rectangle, or polygon listed on lines 15 through 17, they will be directed to the default.html page as defined in the href attribute for the default area.

Closes the <map> element and ends the map.

Figure 4.12 Shapes for Clickable Areas in Image Maps

Creating Image Maps

◎◎ Adding Audio and Video

The use of multimedia—audio and video—on the Web is fairly recent, mainly because the network connection speeds of most Web surfers has not been fast enough to accommodate the large audio and video files. Until about 2001, most Web users, including many small businesses, connected to the Internet through a dial-up modem connection, which is fairly slow. Over the past couple of years, many users have switched to faster connection methods, like DSL and cable modems. These connection options have become cheaper and more readily available in many locations, making them a much more attractive choice than dial-up. Users who have these faster connections can enjoy the new audio and video Web content at a reasonable speed.

The other problem currently facing Web-based multimedia is lack of browser support for many of the common formats. Web browsers have built-in support for viewing the content of XHTML pages. The browser knows how to present content that is described using different elements—for example, it knows how to make text bold or italic. It also knows how to display Web graphic formats, like GIF and JPEG files, without the user having to do anything. For most formats, the user will have to download and install a plug-in program that works in conjunction with the Web browser to display or play these formats. For users with slow connections, downloading these plug-in files can take hours and requires additional hard drive space on the user's computer.

Popular Web Audio and Video File Formats

Like image files, audio and video files can be stored in a number of formats (Figure 4.13). But not all computers can use all formats, so make sure that your audience can use the format that you choose.

☆WARNING   **Audio and Video Files May Require Additional Software**

Many of the audio and video file types are not viewable by all browsers by default. For many of the newer multimedia formats, you must install separate programs in order to run some file types. These programs can be configured as plug-ins that your browser can launch automatically.

Keep this in mind as you develop your documents. Make sure you always develop for the lowest common denominator so that all who view your pages will be able to view the content.

Linking Audio and Video Files to Web Pages

Audio and video files can be added to Web pages in a number of ways. The easiest way is by using the <a> element. Using the <a> element allows a user to click on a link to load the multimedia file. The file is not added as part of the page. For example, if you want to load a video clip directly into your Web page, using the <a> element will not work. However, using links is a very popular method of adding multimedia content to a Web page.

Because there is not yet one widely adopted standard for audio and video, developers store multimedia files in a number of formats, then provide users with links to the files. Figure 4.14 shows the code for creating a Web page that contains links to a video in a number of formats. Figure 4.15 shows the Web page.

Adding Audio and Video

File Type	File Extension	Description
Portable Document Format	pdf	The PDF file format was developed by Adobe Systems, Inc. It uses the PostScript printer language. PDF documents can be viewed via a free client viewer Adobe makes available on its Web site. The software that is needed to create PDF files is a commercial product.
Audio Video Interleave	avi	AVI was developed for storing video files by Microsoft and is supported in all Windows releases, starting with Windows 95. Non-Windows computers may have problems viewing these types of files.
Moving Pictures Expert Group	mpg, mpeg, mp3	MPEG is the most widely supported file type for multimedia on the Web today. It is compatible with all types of computers and is supported by most recent Web browsers.
Real Video	rm, ram	RealVideo format was developed by Real Media for streaming audio and video over the Web. This format was developed to work with lower bandwidth connections, so users with a slower dial-up connection are able to view this type of media, but the quality is lower than other formats.
Shockwave or Flash	swf	The Flash format was developed by Macromedia for multimedia content. The newest versions of Internet Explorer and Netscape ship with built-in support for this format.
QuickTime	qt, mov	QuickTime was developed by Apple Computer. The QuickTime player is required to view these files, but it is distributed free for Windows and Macintosh computers.
Waveform	wav	The wave file format was created by Microsoft and can be played by almost any audio program. Wave files are usually small and contain short sounds, like beeps or bells. This is the audio format that Windows uses for all of its Windows operating system sounds.

Figure 4.13 Common Audio and Video File Formats

Adding Audio and Video

```
1   <?xml version="1.0" ?>
2   <!DOCTYPE html PUBLIC "-//W3C//DTD XHTML 1.0 Strict//EN"
3       "http://www.w3.org/TR/xhtml1/DTD/xhtml1-strict.dtd">
4   <html xmlns="http://www.w3.org/1999/xhtml">
5       <head>
6           <title>Sample Image</title>
7       </head>
8       <body>
9           <div class="center">
10              <h2>My first Christmas</h2>
11              <br />
12              <img src="baby.jpg" alt="Baby Picture" />
13              <br />
14              Click on one of the links below to see a video of
15              my first Christmas:<br />
16              <ul>
17                  <li><a href="christmas.qt">QuickTime format</a></li>
18                  <li><a href="christmas.avi">AVI format</a></li>
19                  <li><a href="christmas.mpeg">MPEG format</a></li>
20              </ul>
21              <br />
22          </div>
23      </body>
24  </html>
```

Figure 4.14 XHTML multmed.html
File with Links to Audio and Video Files

Figure 4.15 XHTML
multmed.html File with
Audio and Video Links in
Browser

Using the `<object>` *element*

You can use the `<object>` element to include inline audio and video files directly in the page. The `<object>` element works much like the `<img>` element; only it can be used to embed any number of file types, including multimedia files. To use the `<object>` element, you must know the content type of the file you are embedding. *Content type* refers to the **Multipurpose Internet Mail Extensions** (MIME) type of the file (see links at the end of this chapter for more information about MIME). Following is the basic syntax for the `<object>` element:

```
<object data="Christmas.mpeg" type="application/mpeg" />
```

Although the `<object>` element has a number of attributes, none are specifically required by the DTD. In the example above, the `data` attribute references the file to be loaded and the `type` attribute tells the browser what kind of file it is. In this case, the file being loaded is an MPEG video file. The `<object>` element can be used just as the `<img>` element is used to load GIF and JPEG images. Following is how you would use the `<object>` element to load an image just like the `<img>` element:

`<img>` element:
```
<img src="baby.jpg" alt="Baby Picture" />
```

`<object>` element:
```
<object data="baby.jpg" type="image/jpeg" />
```

The `<object>` element can also be used to load programs, like Java applets and other executable content, as long as the browser supports it. Below is the code to create a calendar with the current day marked, as seen in Figure 4.16.

```
<object classid="clsid:8E27C92B-1264-101C-8A2F-040224009C02">
   <param name="BackColor" value="14544622" />
   <param name="DayLength" value="1" />
</object>
```

(This example was taken from the w3schools.com Web site. The link is provided at the end of this chapter.)

> ☆**TIP**   The `<object>` Element
>
> In future releases of XHTML, the `<object>` element will probably replace the `<img>` element as the preferred means of displaying graphic content. However, the `<img>` element will probably still be supported in Web browsers for years.

Adding Audio and Video

Figure 4.16 `<object>` Example, Calendar

☆ Summary

▷ Images are included on Web pages using the `<img>` element.

▷ The two standard image file formats are GIF and JPEG.

▷ PNG is an image format for the Web that contains more colors than GIF, but it has not gained wide acceptance.

▷ The `<img>` element has two required attributes, `alt` and `src`.

▷ To make an image a link, contain the `<img>` element within the `<a>` element.

▷ Image maps are images that link to different places depending on where you click within the image.

▷ Image maps have three shapes that can be defined for clickable areas: circle, rectangle, and polygon.

▷ Audio and video can be added to a Web page using the `<a>` or `<object>` element.

▷ The `<object>` element can be used to link any file type into a Web page.

☆ Online References

Devguru `<img>` tag
http://www.devguru.com/Technologies/xhtml/quickref/xhtml_img.html

W3C JPEG site
http://www.w3.org/Graphics/JPEG/

W3C GIF site
http://www.w3.org/Graphics/GIF/spec-gif87.txt

PNG site
http://www.libpng.org/pub/png/

W3C PNG site
http://www.w3.org/Graphics/PNG/

W3C PNG vs. GIF
http://www.w3.org/2001/06tips/png-gif

W3C image map site
Web Accessibility Initiative (WAI)
http://www.w3.org/WAI/
http://www.w3.org/Amaya/User/ImageMaps.html

W3schools.com Web media tutorial
http://www.w3schools.com/media/default.asp

W3schools.com MIME reference
http://www.w3schools.com/media/media_mimeref.asp

Internet Engineering Task Force (IETF) MIME RFC document
http://www.ietf.org/rfc/rfc2045.txt

W3schools.com `<object>` element examples
http://www.w3schools.com/media/media_object.asp

☆ Review Questions

1. What is an inline image?

2. What are the two most popular Web image file formats and which would you use for a photograph?

3. Describe the two required attributes for the `<img>` attribute.

4. Why is the `alt` attribute for `<img>` important for text-based browsers?

5. What two pieces are needed to create an image map?

6. What is the purpose of the default area in an image map?

7. What are two common video formats being used on the Web today?

8. How would you use the `<a>` element to include a video file on your page?

9. How would you use the `<object>` element to include a video file on your page?

☆ Hands-On Exercises

1. Create the `<img>` element code and style sheet properties for an image with the following properties:

   a. Image name sunset.jpg

   b. Alternative text "Picture of a sunset"

   c. Desired number of pixels padding the top and bottom of image, 20 pixels

   d. Pixel width of border, 4 pixels

2. Create an image map using the balloons.gif image provided on this book's Web site that makes the entire red-and-blue balloon part of the clickable area (like the yellow balloon). Use the code in Figure 4.12 as a starting point.

3. Create a Web page that includes a link using the `<a>` element to a sound file. If you are using a Windows computer, you can search your hard drive for .wav files. If you are using a different type of computer, you can search the Web for any of the file types described in this chapter and download a sample sound. (Be careful to read the copyright information on the site before using the sound file.)

4. Use the sound file from Exercise 3 to include the sound as an `<object>`. Be sure to check the MIME type for your file type.

5. Use the example code for Figure 4.16 to create a calendar object. Use a style sheet to center the calendar on the page and put a border around it. Just include the `<object>` element and its content in an XHTML page and open the page in your browser.

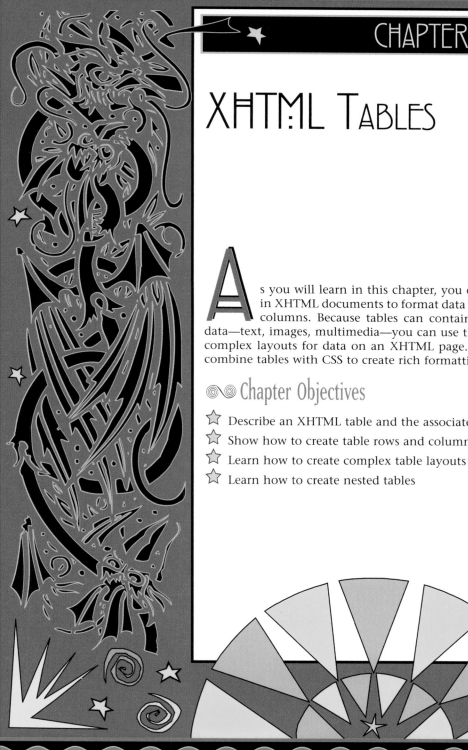

CHAPTER FIVE

XHTML Tables

A s you will learn in this chapter, you can use tables in XHTML documents to format data into rows and columns. Because tables can contain any type of data—text, images, multimedia—you can use them to create complex layouts for data on an XHTML page. You can also combine tables with CSS to create rich formatting features.

Chapter Objectives

★ Describe an XHTML table and the associated elements
★ Show how to create table rows and columns
★ Learn how to create complex table layouts
★ Learn how to create nested tables

◎◎ Working with Tables

This section covers **XHTML tables**, which are sets of elements used to format content, or even an entire document, into rows and columns. The table can contain any type of content, including text, links, images, and multimedia.

The `<table>` and `<caption>` Elements

Tables in XHTML work much the way they do in a spreadsheet or word processing application and resemble a grid. The entire table is surrounded by the **start table tag**, `<table>`, and the **end table tag**, `</table>`. You choose how many rows and columns you need for your table or layout, and then create them using the elements described in this section.

The `<caption>` element is an optional element, and when present, must come directly after the open `<table>` tag. There can only be one `<caption>` element per table. The `<caption>` element is used to describe the data in the table. This element is predominantly used with nonvisual user agents to help users better understand the content of the table.

Table Headings

The **table heading element**, `<th>`, is used to label the rows and columns of a table. This element is an optional element for tables, as some tables do not require headings. In most browsers, the `<th>` element automatically centers the content of the element within the table's cell and makes the text bold. Following is a table heading:

```
<th>Address</th>
```

Rows and Columns

The main body of a table is made up of rows and columns, like a grid. In XHTML, you construct your table one row at a time. Each row begins with an opening **table row**, `<tr>`, **tag**. Each column within that row contains the open and end tags for the **table data**, `<td>`, **element**. After the last `<td>` element is closed for the last column, the row ends with the ending `</tr>` tag. Following is a row with three columns:

```
<tr>
    <td>Column 1</td>
    <td>Column 2</td>
    <td>Column 3</td>
</tr>
```

Simple Table Example

Figure 5.1 is an example of a table with three rows and three columns. This example will show you how the table is laid out in the XHTML document. Figure 5.2

shows this document in a browser. Each column has a header in the first row, and each of the columns and rows are labeled by the content.

Figure 5.4 shows what this XHTML file looks like in Internet Explorer.

```
1   <?xml version="1.0"?>
2   <!DOCTYPE html PUBLIC "-//W3C//DTD XHTML 1.0 Strict//EN"
        "http://www.w3.org/TR/xhtml1/DTD/xhtml1-strict.dtd">
3   <html xmlns="http://www.w3.org/1999/xhtml">
4       <head>
5           <title>Table Example in XHTML</title>
6       </head>
7       <body>
8           <div style="align:center"><h1>Our First Table</h1></div>
9           <!-- Begin Table -->
10          <table border="1">
11              <caption>A Simple Table of Columns and Rows</caption>
12              <!-- Begin First Row -->
13              <tr>
14                  <th>Column 1</th>
15                  <th>Column 2</th>
16                  <th>Column 3</th>
17              </tr>
18              <!-- End First Row -->
19              <!-- Begin Second Row -->
20              <tr>
21                  <td>Column 1 <br /> Row 2</td>
22                  <td>Column 2 <br /> Row 2</td>
23                  <td>Column 3 <br /> Row 2</td>
24              </tr>
25              <!-- End Second Row -->
26              <!-- Begin Third Row -->
27              <tr>
28                  <td>Column 1 <br /> Row 3</td>
29                  <td>Column 2 <br /> Row 3</td>
30                  <td>Column 3 <br /> Row 3</td>
31              </tr>
32              <!-- End Third Row -->
33          </table>
34          <!-- End Table -->
35      </body>
36  </html>
```

Figure 5.1 Simple Table Example

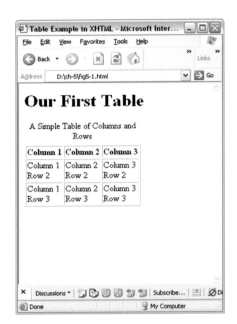

Figure 5.2 Simple Table Example in Internet Explorer

◎◎ Formatting Tables

Labeling Table Sections with `<thead>`, `<tbody>`, and `<tfoot>`

The `<thead>`, `<tbody>`, and `<tfoot>` elements can be used to define logical sections of a table. These elements are used to group the various rows in a table into a header (`<thead>`), body (`<tbody>`), and footer (`<tfoot>`) section. These elements are not widely used today, but will become more prevalent as user agents become more dependent on document structure. They can also be used with style sheets to define formatting properties for various sections of the table.

These elements are optional, but when they are used, they must appear in the following order: `<thead>`, `<tfoot>`, `<tbody>`. The `<tfoot>` element must come after the ending tag for the `</thead>` and before the open tag for the `<tbody>` element, even though its content will be displayed at the bottom of the table in a browser. You'll see how these elements are used in the examples later in this chapter.

Formatting Attributes for Table Elements

The various table elements have a number of attributes that can be used to customize the look and layout of tables, rows, and cells. As with other elements, XHTML Strict does not allow all of the formatting attributes that XHTML Transitional and Frameset allow. Below are the most common attributes that can be used with the `<table>`, `<tr>`, and `<td>` elements.

Attribute Name	Description and Values
`<table>` Element	
`summary`	Text description of the table. Useful for nonvisual browsers.
`width`	Sets the width of the table. Values: Percentage or pixels
`border`	Sets the width of the border around the table. Values: A value of 0 makes the border invisible. An integer value greater than 0 will result in a border size of that number of pixels.
`cellpadding`	Sets the amount of space between the border of the table cell and the data contained in the cell. Values: Percentage or pixels
`cellspacing`	Sets the amount of space between cells. Values: Percentage or pixels
`frame`	Defines which sides of the table will be displayed. Values: ✦ `above`—Top side is visible. ✦ `below`—Bottom side is visible. ✦ `border`—All sides are visible. ✦ `box`—All sides are visible. ✦ `lhs`—Left-hand side is visible. ✦ `hsides`—Top and bottom sides are both visible. ✦ `rhs`—Right-hand side is visible. ✦ `vsides`—Right and left sides are both visible. ✦ `void`—No sides are visible. This is the default value.
`rules`	Defines which rule lines will be displayed. Values: ✦ `all`—Rules will appear between all rows and columns. ✦ `cols`—Rules will be visible between columns only. ✦ `groups`—Rules will be visible between row and column groups. ✦ `none`—The default. No rules are visible. ✦ `rows`—Rules will be visible between rows only.
`<tr>` Element	
`align`	Horizontal alignment of data in all cells in a row Values: `left`, `center`, `right`, `justified`
`valign`	Vertical alignment of data in all cells in a row Values: `top`, `middle`, `bottom`

Figure 5.3 Attributes for Table Elements (*continues*)

Formatting Tables

Attribute Name	Description and Values
`<td>` and `<th>` Elements	
align	Horizontal alignment of data in a cell Values: left, center, right, justified
valign	Vertical alignment of data in a cell Values: top, middle, bottom
rowspan	Number of rows a cell spans Values: integer greater than 1 and less than or equal to the total number of rows in the table
colspan	Number of columns a cell spans Values: integer greater than 1 and less than or equal to the total number of columns in the table
abbr	Used for an abbreviated version of the content of the cell
axis	Used to assign a cell to a category group
headers	List of cells that provide header information for the current cell based on the values of the id attributes header cells. This list is space delimited.
scope	Provides information indicating for which cells the current header cell provides header information Values: col, colspan, row, rowspan

Figure 5.3 Attributes for Table Elements (*continued*)

◎◎ Table Examples

The best way to learn how to use the table elements is by example. This section contains two XHTML document examples that demonstrate many of the formatting attributes listed in the last section. You will see that tables are very powerful tools for formatting content. There are also excellent examples of ways to use tables for formatting on the Web. Some links to online resources are included at the end of this chapter.

Spanning Several Rows and Columns

Our first example will be of a table with content that spans multiple rows and columns. Figure 5.4 contains the XHTML document and Figure 5.5 shows how this page looks in Internet Explorer.

```
1   <?xml version="1.0"?>
2   <!DOCTYPE html PUBLIC "-//W3C//DTD XHTML 1.0 Strict//EN"
        "http://www.w3.org/TR/xhtml1/DTD/xhtml1-strict.dtd">
3   <html xmlns="http://www.w3.org/1999/xhtml">
4     <head>
6       <title>Spanning Multiple Table Rows and Columns
7         with XHTML Tables</title>
8       <style type="text/css">
9         .teal_bg {
10          background-color: "#669999"
11          }
12        .green_bg {
13          background-color: "#cccc66"
14          }
15        caption {
16          font-weight: bold;
17          font-size: 14pt;
18          text-align: center;
19          color: "#000099"
20          }
21      </style>
22    </head>
23    <body>
24      <!-- Begin Table -->
25      <table border="1" cellpadding="5" class="teal_bg">
26        <caption>Saltwater Aquarium Invoice</caption>
27        <thead>
28        <!-- Begin Header Row -->
29          <tr>
30            <th rowspan="2">Item</th>
31            <th colspan="2">Purchase Details</th>
32            <th rowspan="2">Total Price</th>
33          </tr>
34          <tr>
35            <th>Price</th>
36            <th>Quantity</th>
37          </tr>
38        </thead>
39        <tfoot>
40          <tr align="center">
41            <td colspan="4"><small>Thank you for
                shopping with us.</small></td>
42          </tr>
43        <!-- End First Row -->
44        </tfoot>
```

Figure 5.4 Row and Column Span Table Example (*continues*)

```
45              <tbody>
46                 <!-- Begin First Item -->
47                 <tr>
48                    <th>Blue Angel Fish</th>
49                    <td align="center">$19.95</td>
50                    <td align="center">2</td>
51                    <td align="center">$39.90</td>
52                 </tr>
53                 <!-- End First Item -->
54                 <!-- Begin Second Item -->
55                 <tr>
56                    <th>Sailfin Tang Fish</th>
57                    <td align="center">$34.95</td>
58                    <td align="center">1</td>
59                    <td align="center">$34.95</td>
60                 </tr>
61                 <!-- End Second Item -->
62                 <!-- Begin Third Item -->
63                 <tr>
64                    <th>Clown Fish</th>
65                    <td align="center">$3.95</td>
66                    <td align="center">4</td>
67                    <td align="center">$15.80</td>
68                 </tr>
69                 <!-- End Third Item -->
70                 <!-- Begin Invoice Total -->
71                 <tr class="green_bg">
72                    <td colspan="3"><b>TOTAL</b></td>
73                    <td align="center"><b>$89.75</b></td>
74                 </tr>
75                 <!-- End Invoice Total -->
76              </tbody>
77           </table>
78        </body>
79     </html>
```

Figure 5.4 Row and Column Span Table Example (*continued*)

Nested Tables

The second example demonstrates **nested tables**. A nested table is a table that is contained within another table. Nested tables give XHTML developers even more control over the layout of their content but add an additional level of complexity to the XHTML document code.

Figures 5.6 and 5.7 show a simple example of table nesting to give you some idea of how tables can be used for complex formatting. Figure 5.6 shows the XHTML document and Figure 5.7 shows what it looks like in the browser.

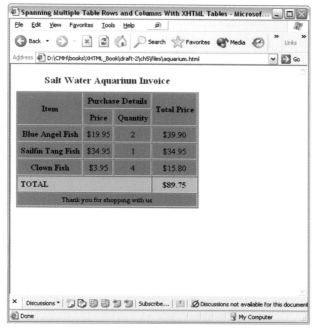

Figure 5.5 Row and Column Span Table Example in Internet Explorer

```
1  <?xml version="1.0"?>
2  <!DOCTYPE html PUBLIC "-//W3C//DTD XHTML 1.0 Strict//EN"
        "http://www.w3.org/TR/xhtml1/DTD/xhtml1-strict.dtd">
3  <html xmlns="http://www.w3.org/1999/xhtml">
4      <head>
5          <title>Spanning Multiple Table Rows and Columns
              with XHTML Tables</title>
6          <style type="text/css">
7              .outer {
8                  background-color: "#999999"
9                  }
10                 .inner {
11                     background-color: "#ff9999"
12                     }
13         </head>
14         <body>
```

Figure 5.6 Nested Table Example (*continues*)

```
15      <!--  Begin Outer Table -->
16      <table border="1" cellpadding="5" class="outer">
17          <caption><strong>Phone Book</strong></caption>
18          <!--  Begin Header Row -->
19          <tr>
20              <th>Name</th>
21              <th>Address</th>
22              <th>Phone Number</th>
23          </tr>
24          <!-- End Header Row -->
25          <!-- Begin First Row -->
26          <tr>
27              <td>Wendy Lee Rogell</td>
28              <td>
29                 <!--  Begin Inner Table -->
30                 <table  border="1" class="inner">
31                   <tr>
32                       <td colspan="3">123 West Liberty Dr.</td>
33                   </tr>
34                   <tr>
35                       <td>San Francisco</td>
36                       <td>CA</td>
37                       <td>94102</td>
38                   </tr>
39                 </table>
40                 <!--  End Inner Table -->
41              </td>
42              <td>(415) 555-1212</td>
43          </tr>
44          <!-- End First Row -->
45          <!-- Begin Second Row -->
46          <tr>
47              <td>Julie Temlak</td>
48              <td>
49                 <!--  Begin Inner Table -->
50                 <table  border="1" class="inner">
51                   <tr>
52                       <td colspan="3">456 Lighthouse Way</td>
53                   </tr>
54                   <tr>
55                       <td>Providence</td>
56                       <td>RI</td>
57                       <td>02901</td>
58                   </tr>
59                 </table>
60                 <!--  End Inner Table -->
```

Figure 5.6 Nested Table Example (*continues*)

```
61                </td>
62                <td>(415) 555-1212</td>
63            </tr>
64            <!-- End Second Row -->
65        </table>
66    </body>
67 </html>
```

Figure 5.6 Nested Table Example (*continued*)

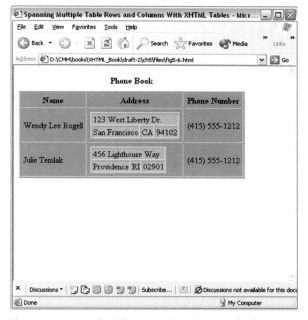

Figure 5.7 Nested Table Example in Internet Explorer

In Figure 5.7, the data in the outer table is gray, and the data in the nested tables is pink. Notice that the nested tables are completely contained within one data cell of the outer (gray) table.

☆ Summary

▷ The open `<table>` tag has a number of attributes that can be used to format the table.

▷ Table headings, `<th>`, and table data, `<td>`, elements both represent single cells in a table.

▷ The sections of a table can be labeled with the `<thead>`, `<tbody>`, and `<tfoot>` elements.

▷ Style sheets can be used to format the table and the data inside of a table's cells.

▷ The attributes `rowspan` and `colspan` can be used to format table cells to span one or more row or column.

▷ A nested table is a table that exists completely within the cell of another table.

☆ Online References

W3C tables overview
`http://www.w3.org/TR/html401/struct/tables.html`

Guide to Standards-Compliant XHTML Tables
`http://velvetant.org/guide/tables.html`

XHTML tables
`http://www.topxml.com/xhtml/articles/xhtml_tables/`

XHTML tables module—W3C
`http://www.w3.org/TR/xhtml2/mod-tables.html`

Lean and Mean Tables
`http://hotwired.lycos.com/webmonkey/98/43/index4a.html`

☆ Review Questions

1. What is the purpose of the `<caption>` element?
2. Which table element automatically centers text and creates a bold type?
3. What are the differences between `<th>` and `<td>`?
4. Which `<table>` attribute determines the amount of space between table cells?
5. How would you center the content inside a single cell?
6. How would you change the background color for an entire row?
7. What attribute would you use if you wanted a cell to span three columns? Which element would this attribute be placed inside?
8. How many cells of the outer table does a nested table occupy?

☆ Hands-On Exercises

1. Create the simple table example from Figure 5.2 and view the document in a browser. Use a style sheet to provide formatting properties.

2. Based on the document you created in Exercise 1, add `<thead>`, `<tfoot>`, and `<tbody>` elements to the appropriate areas of your table.

3. Create the XHTML document for the following Daycare Child ID Card Web page (you can use any image that you like) with a single table layout. Following are a few hints:

   a. The code for the purple background is 993366 (dark blue for boys is 000066).

   b. The code for the gray background is 666666.

   c. Use a style sheet to format the colors and text properties.

   d. Use the `cellpadding` attribute to create the space around the cell data.

   e. Use `rowspan` and `colspan` for the "Identification Card" header and the picture cell.

4. Using the XHTML document from Exercise 3, create the area of the table that is gray as a nested table.

5. Validate the documents you created in Exercises 3 and 4 on the W3C Validator Web site.

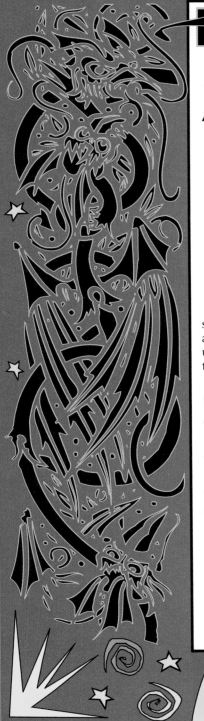

XHTML Frames

Frames are used to create more than one window for data within a single XHTML document. The XHTML 1.0 specification provides a separate version of the specification, known as XHTML Frameset, for creating frame documents. By the end of this chapter, you will understand what frames are, how to lay out a Web page containing frames, and how to create the pieces of the page.

◎◎ Chapter Objectives

☆ Describe how to use XHTML Frameset to create frame pages

☆ Learn how to lay out frames using either pixels or percentages

☆ Learn how to create nested frames

☆ Learn about XFrames, the proposed replacement for the current frames implementation

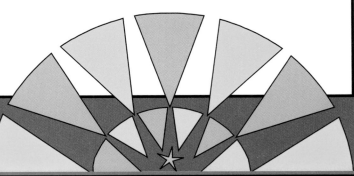

Working with Frames

So far in this book, we have primarily used the XHTML Strict version of the XHTML 1.0 specification. This section will spend some time discussing the **XHTML Frameset** version of the XHTML 1.0 specification and how to incorporate frames into your XHTML documents. Note that neither XHTML Transitional nor XHTML Strict support frames, so make sure you use the correct DTD in your XHTML documents when using frames:

```
<!DOCTYPE html PUBLIC "-//W3C//DTD XHTML 1.0 Frameset//EN"
        "http://www.w3.org/TR/xhtml1/DTD/xhtml1-frameset.dtd">
```

☆**WARNING**   Use of Frames

Although frames provide additional functionality that is not easily attained with regular XHTML, they should be used sparingly, and only when the audience for the content is well defined. Many Web developers dislike frames because they are difficult to maintain and their display can sometimes be unpredictable. Frames are also not a part of the XHTML Strict DTD, which means that frames will likely be deprecated in future versions of XHTML.

Many types of clients, such as Web-enabled phones, handheld PDAs, and text-based browsers, cannot display frames. Also, bookmarking individual pages within a frames document set can be very difficult.

It is highly recommended that you use an alternative like tables or style sheets to achieve a particular formatting functionality instead of frames to ensure that your pages will be compatible with future browsers and other clients.

The purpose of **frames** is to allow developers to divide a browser window into independent pieces. These pieces are sometimes called "frame windows." A frame document is actually made up of many documents: a container document that defines the number of frames the document contains and one or more XHTML documents that will fill the frames the container document creates.

Creating Frame Documents

The **container document** is used to specify the number of frames the document will contain and which files should be displayed within each frame. It lays out the frames in a grid pattern, much like XHTML tables, but unlike tables, the content of the various rows and cells are contained in external files, which are referenced by individual `<frame />` elements. The container document does not contain any data, only elements that define the layout and content documents for the various frames.

Let's start with a simple example. We can use frames to create a document with four individual windows, as seen in Figure 6.1. Two elements are used to describe the frame container:

1. **`<frameset>`** This element defines the document as a frame document, and defines the number of frames being created. As you will notice in the examples, there is no `<body>` element in a frame document. The `<frameset>` element takes the place of `<body>` in a frame document. The individual `<frame />` elements within the document are contained within the `<frameset>` element.

2. **`<frame />`** Each frame in the document will be described by a `<frame />` element. This element is used to identify the name of the document that will be contained within each individual frame and to provide special formatting properties to the frame.

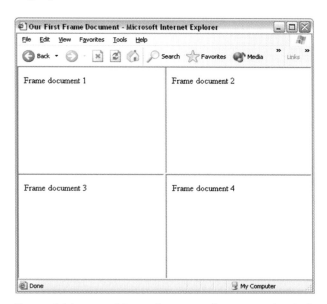

Figure 6.1 Layout of Frame Document frame-container1.xhtml

The XHTML document in Figure 6.2 shows the code to lay out the frame container in Figure 6.1. Keep in mind that there are actually five documents that make up this Web page: frame-container1.html, frame1.html, frame2.html, frame3.html, and frame4.html.

```
1   <?xml version="1.0"?>
2   <!DOCTYPE html PUBLIC "-//W3C//DTD XHTML 1.0 Frameset//EN"
3       "http://www.w3.org/TR/xhtml1/DTD/xhtml1-frameset.dtd">
4   <html xmlns="http://www.w3.org/1999/xhtml">
5       <head>
6           <title>Our First Frame Document</title>
7       </head>
8       <frameset cols="50%,50%" rows="50%,50%">
9           <frame src="frame1.html" />
10          <frame src="frame2.html" />
11          <frame src="frame3.html" />
12          <frame src="frame4.html" />
13      </frameset>
14  </html>
```

Figure 6.2 Layout of Frame Document frame-container1.xhtml

The `<frameset>` Element

The outermost `<frameset>` element can contain one or more `<frame />` or `<frameset>` elements. These inner elements define the layout of the container. In Figure 6.2, notice that the `<frameset>` elements contain rows and cols attributes. These attributes are used to specify the number of rows and/or columns in the frameset. You would expect a document with two rows to set the value of the rows attribute to 2—rows="2"—but this is not the case. The number of rows and columns is determined by the number of items in the comma-separated list of the attribute's value. Each item in the list determines the size in either pixels or as a percentage for each row or column.

In our example, we define two rows, each taking up 50% of the frameset's available space: rows="50%, 50%". If we wanted to define four equal rows in our frameset using percentages, we would assign the value of each row to 25%: rows="25%, 25%, 25%, 25%".

Using percentages to determine the size of each row or column does not give us a great deal of control over the actual size of the frames. There is no way to know how large or small the client's Web browser window will be when the documents is viewed, and the browser will lay out the frames relative to how much space it has. You can use pixel values to control the actual widths of columns and rows. If you were working with a frameset that was exactly 200 pixels wide, and you wanted to create two equal rows, you could use the percentages as we did above, rows="50%, 50%", or you could assign actual pixels, rows="100, 100", which would set the widths to 100. If the frameset's total size changed to 300, these two rows would still be only 100 pixels wide, while the rows defined at 50% would now be 150 pixels wide.

Many times, developers want to make one row or column a set width, and then allocate the rest of the space available to another row or rows. A good example of this is a site that has a menu bar in a column on the left side of the screen and a data window on the right side. The wildcard character, "*", can be used to achieve this affect. Let's look at an example of how this works by creating two frameset documents and seeing how they display in different-sized browser windows.

Figure 6.3 shows the code for our first document, pixel-example.html, which allocates 200 pixels for the left column and then uses the "*" character to allocate the rest of the space to the second frame on the right side. Figure 6.4 shows the code for our second document, percent-example.html, which allocates 50% to each of two rows. Figure 6.5 shows how our first document looks in two differently sized browser windows, and Figure 6.6 shows how our second document looks in the same windows. Notice that the left column in our first document stays the same width, while the first column in the second document changes its width to accommodate the new window size.

```
1   <?xml version="1.0"?>
2   <!DOCTYPE html PUBLIC "-//W3C//DTD XHTML 1.0 Frameset//EN"
3       "http://www.w3.org/TR/xhtml1/DTD/xhtml1-frameset.dtd">
4   <html xmlns="http://www.w3.org/1999/xhtml">
5       <head>
6           <title>Pixel Example</title>
7       </head>
8       <frameset cols="200,*">
9           <frame src="frame1.html" />
10          <frame src="frame2.html" />
11      </frameset>
12  </html>
```

Figure 6.3 pixel-example.html

```
1   <?xml version="1.0"?>
2   <!DOCTYPE html PUBLIC "-//W3C//DTD XHTML 1.0 Frameset//EN"
3       "http://www.w3.org/TR/xhtml1/DTD/xhtml1-frameset.dtd">
4   <html xmlns="http://www.w3.org/1999/xhtml">
5       <head>
6           <title>Percent Example</title>
7       </head>
8       <frameset cols="50%, 50%">
9           <frame src="frame1.html" />
10          <frame src="frame2.html" />
11      </frameset>
12  </html>
```

Figure 6.4 percent-example.html

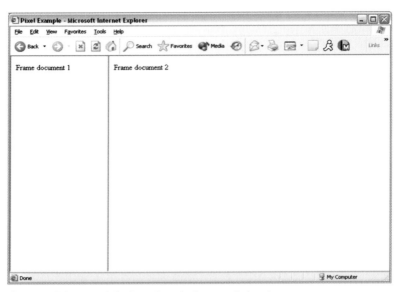

Figure 6.5 Browser Windows for pixel-example.html

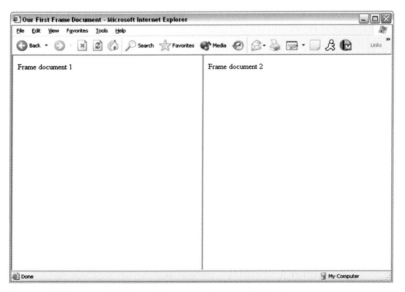

Figure 6.6 Browser Windows for percent-example.html

The `<frame>` Element

As you have probably figured out, the `<frame />` element is used to define where document will display inside each individual frame. The `src` attribute is used like the `href` attribute in the `<a>` element to locate the document. Figure 6.7 describes the other attributes that can be used with the `<frame />` element.

Attribute Name	Description and Values
name	Used to name, or identify, a particular frame within a frameset. This attribute will be replaced with the `id` attribute in future versions. Value: text string
id	Like `name`, this attribute is used to uniquely identify the frame. Unlike the `name` attribute, according to the XHTML specfications the `id` attribute must be unique within a document. Value: text string
longdesc	This attribute is not yet widely supported. The value of this attribute will be a URL that directs clients unable to view frames to an alternate page. Value: URI
src	Contains the URI, usually a URL, that references the document to be displayed in the frame. Value: URI
frameborder	The value of this attribute determines the width, in pixels, of the frame's border. If it is set to 0 (zero), the border is invisible. Value: integer value for number of pixels
marginwidth	Defines the width in pixels of the margin width between frames. Value: percent or pixels
marginheight	Defines the width in pixels of the margin height between frames. Value: percent or pixels
noresize	Setting this attribute will prevent the frame from being resized. By default, the frame, like a window, can be resized by clicking on and dragging the border or corner. This attribute turns off the ability to resize the frame. Value: noresize
scrolling	This attribute controls scrolling of the frame. This attribute can take one of three values: ★ yes—Enables scrolling within the frame. Scroll bars will be visible. ★ no—Scrolling will be disabled within the frame. If the frame contains content that is too large for the frame, the content will be cut off from view. ★ Value: yes (there will be scroll bars), no (there will not be scroll bars) and auto (there will be scroll bars only if needed)

Figure 6.7 Attributes for `<frame>` Element

Nesting Frames

As with tables, you can nest frames within frames by including additional <frameset> elements within the outermost <frameset> element. This allows you to create very complex page layouts. Be aware, however, that frames take longer to render than other XHTML documents because of their complexity.

Let's look at an example. Figure 6.8 contains the code for a complex frame layout. Figure 6.9 shows how this document appears in a Web browser.

```
1   <?xml version="1.0"?>
2   <!DOCTYPE html PUBLIC "-//W3C//DTD XHTML 1.0 Frameset//EN"
3       "http://www.w3.org/TR/xhtml1/DTD/xhtml1-frameset.dtd">
4   <html xmlns="http://www.w3.org/1999/xhtml">
5       <head>
6           <title>Our First Frame Document</title>
7       </head>
8       <frameset cols="25%,50%,25%">
9           <frame src="frame1.html" />
10          <frameset rows="33%, 34%, 33%">
11              <frame src="nested-frame1.html" />
12              <frame src="nested-frame2.html" />
13              <frame src="nested-frame3.html" />
14          </frameset>
15          <frame src="frame2.html" />
16      </frameset>
```

Figure 6.8 Nested Frames (nested-frames.html)

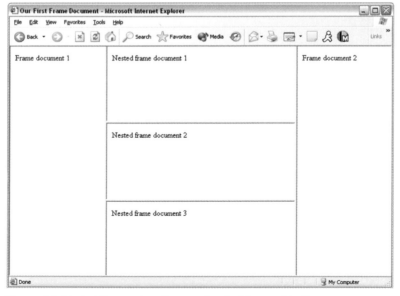

Figure 6.9 Nested Frames in a Browser (nested-frames.html)

In this example, the outermost frameset contains three columns. The middle column contains an additional <frameset> element that defines three more frames in rows. This nested frameset contains the documents nested-frame1.html, nested-frame2.html, and nested-frame3.html.

◎◎ XFrames—The Future of Frames in XML

XFrames is a new technology being developed by the W3C; it is not yet a recommendation. XFrames will be the replacement technology for HTML frames and XHTML Frameset. The latest working draft on XFrames was released in August 2002.

☆ **WARNING**   **XFrames Is a New Technology**

The specification for XFrames is still in draft form, so it is likely to change before being released as a recommendation. Because some of the working drafts developed by the W3C do not receive enough support to become recommendations, it is also possible that this draft will not become a recommendation. Check the W3C Web site before implementing any technology that is not yet a recommendation.

The draft lists several usability issues with the current implementation of frames:

☆ The "back" button in a browser works unintuitively in many cases.

☆ Users cannot bookmark documents in a frameset.

☆ The "reload" button in a browser has unpredictable results and often will not reload the frameset exactly as it was.

☆ Searching frame documents is difficult because searching finds XHTML pages, not frame pages. This means that search results usually return the individual XHTML pages, not the frameset document, so users are left without the navigation context that they expected.

☆ Search engines are examples of user agents that do not support frames.

☆ Since frame documents can point to any URL, relative or absolute, there are security problems caused by the fact that the user cannot tell when frame documents come from sources that are not secure.

XFrames promises to fix many of these issues by providing a more robust set of functionality that will allow developers to take advantage of the benefits that frames provide, while eliminating the navigation and security issues that have caused complaints.

XFrames—The Future of Frames in XML

☆ Summary

➤ Frames can be used to separate a Web browser window into multiple, independent windows.

➤ In XHTML, you must include the XHTML Frameset DTD to use frames.

➤ Frames can be nested within other frames to create complex layouts.

➤ The rows and cols attributes for individual frames can be referenced in pixels or percentages.

➤ Use pixels to determine sizes of frames when you want the size to be fixed.

➤ Use percentages to determine the sizes of frames when you want the frames to resize dynamically, depending on the size of the user's browser window.

➤ Use the wildcard character, "*," to dynamically size frames based on the size of the user's browser window.

☆ Online References

W3C frames document (for HTML)
`http://www.w3.org/TR/REC-html40/present/frames.html`

Introduction to frames
`http://wp.netscape.com/assist/net_sites/frames.html`

Search engines and frames
`http://searchenginewatch.com/webmasters/article.php/2167901`

Frames in HTML documents
`http://www.w3.org/TR/REC-html40/present/frames.html`

W3C XFrames working draft
`http://www.w3.org/TR/xframes/`

☆ Review Questions

1. What are some of the issues with using frames with new Web clients like phones and PDAs?

2. In a frame document, which element describes the properties of an individual window?

3. Describe what the rows and cols attributes represent.

4. What is the difference between using pixels and percentages to size frames?

5. What are the advantages of nesting frames?

6. Describe how frames could be used to create a table of contents that does not scroll.

7. What XML technology will likely replace frames?

☆ Hands-On Exercises

1. Create a frameset document with three equal frames that span the document vertically, as shown below. Use percentages to set the width of the frames.

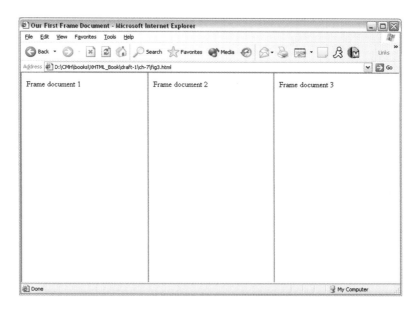

2. Create the document shown in Exercise 1, but set the first column to a fixed width of 150 pixels, the second to 25% of the window, and the third to the remaining window space.

3. Create the document shown in Exercise 1, but create the middle frame as a nested frame.

4. Create the frame layout shown below. The middle row of three frames is nested. You can use either pixels or percentages for the sizing.

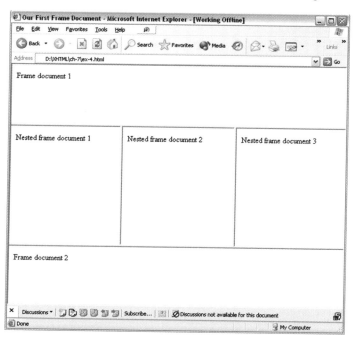

5. Research the current version of XFrames on the W3C Web site. Provide a brief summary of the benefits that it will provide over the current implementation of frames.

XHTML Forms

One of the features that separate the Web from traditional media such as television, radio, magazines, and newspapers is the ability of users to interact with the Web site. This interactivity allows Web site owners to collect data from their visitors, conduct surveys, and sell products or services. Even the familiar search box is an example of this interactivity that gives Web users the ability to communicate with Web page owners and even to customize their experience in some cases. In this chapter, you'll learn how to make Web pages interactive using XHTML forms.

Chapter Objectives

☆ Describe the purpose and use of XHTML forms

☆ Understand how Web servers process form data

☆ Learn about the different XHTML form elements

☆ Discover how to use the elements' attributes to customize form input

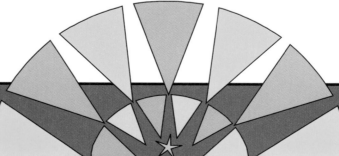

◎◎ XHTML Forms

One of the features that separate the Web from traditional media such as television, radio, magazines, and newspapers is the ability of users to interact with the Web site. This interactivity allows Web site owners to collect data from their visitors, conduct surveys, and sell products or services. Even the familiar search box is an example of this interactivity that gives Web users the ability to communicate with Web page owners and even to customize their experience in some cases. In this chapter, you'll learn how to make Web pages interactive with XHTML forms.

◎◎ The Basics of Web-Based Forms

The XHTML elements that you will learn about in this chapter have been an integral part of the HTML language for many years. Almost every Web browser and Web server currently in use today supports **forms**, and to some extent most of the new client devices such as cell phones and PDAs support forms as well.

A form can contain many types of input elements, including text boxes, password boxes, buttons, checkboxes, and pull-down menus. JavaScript can be used to test the values entered in the various form fields or to populate a field with a value based on input in other fields. For example, it can be used to ensure that a phone number field contains numbers instead of letters. JavaScript is not a part of XHTML and is beyond the scope of this book, but you can find more information using the links listed at the end of this chapter.

After filling out a form, the user usually presses a "Submit" button, which sends the data to be processed by a program that resides on the Web server. This program will send back a confirmation page or redirect the user to a new Web page. For example, the form's data may be written to a database or used to format an email message. These programs execute on the server and can be written in any language supported by the Web server, such as Perl, C++ or Java.

> ☆**TIP**   **Form-Processing Programs**
>
> Form-processing programs are beyond the scope of this book, but you can get more information using the links provided at the end of this chapter. A form-processing script called **cgiemail** is provided free of charge by the Massachusetts Institute of Technology (MIT). This script takes the input from a form and sends it to a specified email address. Following is the Web address for this script:
>
> `http://web.mit.edu/wwwdev/cgiemail/`
>
> Anyone is free to download and use the script. The Web site provides detailed instructions on how to install and use the script. Check with your Web hosting provider or system administrator to see if they will allow you to install this program. Most Web hosting companies provide their users with a form-processing script that will send the data submitted in a form to their users' email addresses.

The Basics of Web-Based Forms

◎◉ Form Elements

The <form> Element

A form can be located anywhere in the body of an XHTML document. A Web page can contain more than one form, but forms cannot be nested. All form elements are contained within the <form> **element** between the opening <form> and closing </form> tags. Other XHTML elements can be contained within the <form> element as well, but only the form-specific elements that you will learn about shortly will be used to send data to the processing program.

The action *attribute*

The <form> start tag has only one required attribute, the action **attribute**. This attribute provides the path to the program on the server that will process the form's data when the user presses the "Submit" button. The value of action can be either an absolute or relative URL, or it can contain the mailto: action, which will send the form data to an email address. Following are examples of the <form> element with the action attribute defined:

1. **Relative URL:**

   ```
   <form action="/cgi-bin/process.cgi">
   ```

   In the first example, the value of action is a relative URL to a program that resides in the cgi-bin directory of the same Web server on which the form XHTML page is located. The file process.cgi is the program that will receive the form's data when the user submits the form.

   The value of action is a relative URL to a program that resides in the cgi-bin directory of the same Web server on which the form XHTML page is located. The file process.cgi is the program that will receive the form's data when the user submits the form.

2. **Absolute URL:**

   ```
   <form action="http://www.chughes.com/cgi-bin/process.cgi">
   ```

   The second example uses the same process.cgi program as the target for the form's data, but in this case, the program's URL is an absolute URL. In this case, your form's data is being sent to a program that resides on a different Web server.

   In both examples, the process.cgi file is the program that processes the form's data. This program can be written to perform a number of tasks on the data that is collected from a form:

   ☆ Store or update the data in a database.

   ☆ Use it as search criteria.

   ☆ Take an order for a service or product.

   ☆ Create a new Web page based on the data submitted.

Form Elements

Once the data has been processed, the program then usually sends a response back to the user. The user may be directed to another Web page, perhaps one that thanks them for their submission, or a page is returned as the result of what the user entered in the form. For example, if you type a keyword in a search box, the page that is returned is a list of items that match the criteria you asked for.

3. **The** `mailto:` **action:**

```
<form action="mailto:cheryl@chughes.com">
```

The third example is the `mailto:` value for the `action` attribute. This is a special keyword for a form that instructs the browser to run the email program on the local machine. It does not require any processing by the Web server, but it does require that an email program be located on the user's computer. If the user's computer does not have a default email program installed, the form will not work using the `mailto:` action. This means that the form's submission may or may not work on every computer.

The `method` *attribute*

The other attribute that is usually defined in the `<form>` element, but not explicitly required, is the **`method` attribute**. This attribute tells the Web server how the form's data is to be sent to the program specified by the `action` attribute. The two values for `method` are `get` and `post`, with `get` being defined as the default value.

☆**TIP**   **The `get` Value for the Method Attribute**

The `get` value is the default value for the `method` attribute. That is, if you do not include this attribute in your XHTML code, then the server will automatically assign `get` as the method. This means that the two examples below are equivalent and will both use the `get` method to send the form's data to the Web server:

```
<form action="/cgi-bin/process.cgi" method="get">
<form action="/cgi-bin/process.cgi">
```

The Web server uses the values of `get` and `post` to determine how it receives the data. The `post` method tells the Web browser to send the data back to the server as regular data. The `get` method tells the Web browser to append the data from the form to the end of a URL. This method is commonly used for search engines so that users are able to bookmark or send the URL of the results. For example, if we wanted to search Google for XHTML books, we would first go to the Google Web site at the following:

```
http://www.google.com
```

We would then enter our search string into Google's search box, as shown in Figure 7.1.

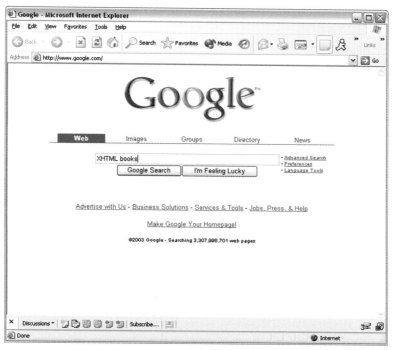

Figure 7.1 Google.com Search Page with "XHTML books" Entered as Search Term

After we submit the search, Google returns a page with links to books about XHTML, as seen in Figure 7.2. Look at the URL in the address bar of the browser:

```
http://www.google.com/search?hl=en&ie=UTF-8&oe=UTF-8&q=
xhtml+books ———[ Data submitted in get request ]———
```

Notice that a long string of data is appended to the URL. The part of the URL that comes after the question mark is the data submitted by the form. This data is highlighted in red. Notice that at the end of the URL is our search criteria: q=XHTML+books. We can now bookmark this URL or email the URL to someone who would be interested in this page of results. Because the post method sends the data directly back to the Web server, nothing is appended to the URL, so the results from a form that is posted cannot be bookmarked.

Figure 7.2 Google.com Search Results Page for "XHTML books" Search Term

A number of elements can be used on XHTML forms to provide the means for users to enter data or choose options. All of the input elements must be contained between the `<form>` and `</form>` tags. This next section covers the various input elements and shows you how to use them.

Text Input Elements

Text input elements allow users to enter text into a field on a form. Three text elements are specified within the `<input />` element by the `type` attribute:

☆ Text: `<input type="text" />`

☆ Password: `<input type="password" />`

☆ File: `<input type="file" />`

The `text` input box allows a user to enter data into a single-line field. The `password` box also allows data to be entered into a single line, but replaces the text being typed with asterisks to hide the actual input characters. The `file` type allows a user to browse the hard drive to select a file to submit.

☆**WARNING**   **Data Entered into** `password` **Field Is Not Secure**

Even though the `password` input field masks the data being entered with asterisks, this does not mean that the data is secure. If the form is submitted on a nonsecure Web site, or if the form uses the get method to submit the data, the data that is entered into the password field will be visible in plain text. To ensure the security of data entered into a `password` form field, make sure the form is submitted over a secure Web connection and use the `post` method to send the data back to the server.

Attributes for Text Input Elements

A number of attributes can be used within the `<input>` element for text fields, as shown in Figure 7.3.

Attribute	Description
`maxlength`	Maximum number of characters allowed for input
`name`	Used to identify the input field
`size`	Defines the size of the input field in characters. If this is smaller than the maxlength attribute, the field will scroll.
`type`	Defines the type of input (text, password, or file for text input fields)
`disabled`	Disables the field for user input. The value of a disabled field will not be sent to the processing program.
`readonly`	Makes the content of the text field unchangeable. The value of this field will be sent to the processing program.
`value`	Sets a default value
`onselect`	For use with scripts. An event handle that specifies an action to be performed when the field is selected.
`onchange`	For use with scripts. An event handle that specifies an action to be performed when the content of the field has been changed.

Figure 7.3 Text Input Element Attributes

When a form is submitted, the data is sent to the server in the form of **name value pairs**. Each form element has a name that identifies the item, specified in the `name` attribute. The value of the element is the data that the user provides. For example, the following form element's name is `ZipCode`. If the user entered "02109" in the text box, then `02109` becomes the value. The pair, `ZipCode=02109`, is sent to the server.

```
<input type="text" name="ZipCode"  />
```

Let's look at some examples. Figure 7.4 shows the XHTML code for a form with examples of each of these input elements and various attributes. Figure 7.5 shows this document in a browser.

```
1    <h4>Enter your name:</h4>
2    <input type="text" name="name" size="35" />
3    <h4>Enter your password:</h4>
4    <input type="password" name="password" size="35" />
```

Figure 7.4 Text Element Form Example

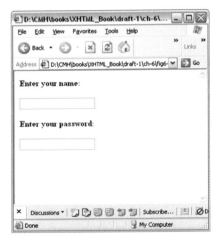

Figure 7.5 Text Element Form Example in Browser

The `<textarea>` Element

The `<textarea>` element also provides a text-based field for users to type in data. Unlike the text input fields described above, the `<textarea>` element creates a multiline input box. The `rows` and `cols` attributes for `<textarea>` define the number of rows and columns the text box will contain. Also unlike the empty `<input />` element, the `<textarea>` element has a start and an end tag. Any data contained within the start and end tags will appear in the text box and be sent to the server as the value of the `<textarea>` element.

Attributes for `<textarea>` Element

The `<textarea>` element has a number of attributes in addition to `rows` and `cols`. The attribute `readonly` makes the text area only readable, meaning that the user cannot change the data in the box. This feature is commonly used for agreements and disclaimers. These attributes are summarized in Figure 7.6.

Attribute	Description
name	Used to identify the input field
rows	Number of horizontal rows of the text area
cols	Number of vertical columns of the text area
readonly	Makes the content of the text area unchangeable
disabled	Disables the field for user input. The value of a disabled field will not be sent to the processing program.
readonly	Makes the content of the text field unchangeable. The value of this field will be sent to the processing program.
onselect	For use with scripts. An event handle that specifies an action to be performed when the field is selected.
onchange	For use with scripts. An event handle that specifies an action to be performed when the content of the field has been changed.

Figure 7.6 `<textarea>` Input Element Attributes

Figure 7.7 shows a few examples. Figure 7.8 shows how they look in a browser.

```
1   <h4>Text Area Example 1:</h4>
2   <textarea name="example1" rows="5" cols="15"></textarea>
```

```
1   <h4>Text Area Example 2 (includes default text):</h4>
2   <textarea name="example2" rows="5" cols="35">Sample
    text. This text will show up inside the text area
    box.</textarea>
```

```
1   <h4>Text Area Example 3 (includes default text that is
    read only):</h4>
2   <textarea name="example2" rows="10" cols="35"
    readonly="readonly">Sample text. This text will show
3   up inside the text area box. Because this text area is
    read-only, this text cannot
4   be modified by the user.</textarea>
```

Figure 7.7 `<textarea>` Element Form Examples

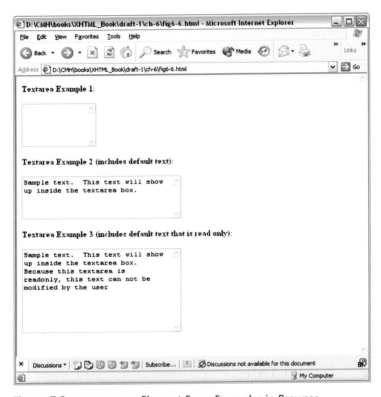

Figure 7.8 `<textarea>` Element Form Examples in Browser

Selection Form Elements

The **selection form elements** allow the user to select one or many choices from a list. Like text elements, the following selection elements are specified within the `<input />` element by the `type` attribute:

☆ Checkboxes: `<input type="checkbox" />`

☆ Radio buttons: `<input type="radio" />`

The third type of selection element is the drop-down list:

☆ Drop-down lists: `<select> </select>`

Checkboxes and Radio Buttons

Checkboxes are used for lists where the user can choose one or more selections from a list of options. Each item in a checkbox group can be checked or unchecked. Checkboxes are usually denoted by a square box that contains an X when selected. When the form is submitted, only the data from the checked items is sent to the server. Because checkboxes can have more than one value, the value that is sent to the server will be a list of the checkboxes that are checked. The ones that are not checked will not have their values sent to the server.

Radio buttons are also used for lists; however, radio buttons allow the user to choose only one item. Radio buttons are usually denoted by a round circle that is filled in when the item is selected. Each item in the radio button group has the same name assigned to its `name` attribute, and only the value of the selected item is sent to the server when the form is submitted.

Both checkboxes and radio buttons are arranged into groups. The `checked` attribute can be set to preselect certain items, meaning that they will be checked by default when the form loads. For checkboxes, multiple items can be prechecked. For radio buttons, only one can be prechecked.

Let's look at an example of each. Figure 7.9 shows a checkbox group that asks users to select which animals they own as pets, and a radio button group asking users to choose their favorite color. Figure 7.10 shows how these would look in a browser.

Checkbox Group
```
1  <h4>Please select each type of pet you own:</h4>
2  <input type="checkbox" name="pets" value="dog" checked="checked"
       />Dog<br />
3  <input type="checkbox" name="pets" value="cat" />Cat<br />
4  <input type="checkbox" name="pets" value="bird" />Bird<br />
5  <input type="checkbox" name="pets" value="llama" />Llama<br />
```

Radio Button Group
```
1  <h4>Please select your favorite color:</h4>
2  <input type="radio" name="color" value="blue" checked="checked"
       />Blue<br />
3  <input type="radio" name="color" value="green" />Green<br />
4  <input type="radio" name="color" value="yellow" />Yellow<br />
5  <input type="radio" name="color" value="orange" />Orange<br />
```

These items have been preset as selected.

Figure 7.9 Checkbox and Radio Button Form Element Examples

Drop-Down Lists Using `<select>`

The `<select>` form element is used to create a **drop-down list** of items. The list appears in a scrollable box. These are usually used for long lists of items. The items that are included in the list are specified by the `<option>` element. Each item is listed in a separate `<option>` element. All of the `<option>` elements are contained between the beginning `<select>` and end `</select>` element tags.

Attributes for the `<select>` *Element*

As with the other form elements, the `name` attribute is used to identify the `<select>` element. The `size` attribute is used to specify how many lines of the drop-down list are visible. The default for `size` is one line. If the `size` attribute is not specified, the default size of one will apply. The `selected` attribute is used to set a default value. To allow the user to select more than one item from the list, the `multiple` attribute can be set. To select more than one item, the user usually

Figure 7.10 Checkbox and Radio Button Form
Element Examples in Browser

holds down the Ctrl or ⇧Shift key while clicking on the desired items. If `multi-ple` is not set, this element functions like a radio button group, allowing only one item from the list to be chosen. Figure 7.11 summarizes the attributes for `<select>`.

Attribute	Description
name	Used to identify the input field
size	Number of lines that are visible in the scroll box
multiple	Specifies whether or not user can choose multiple items
disabled	Disables the field for user input. The value of a disabled field will not be sent to the processing program.
tabindex	Indicates a field's place in the sequence of the tab order
onfocus	For use with scripts. An event handle that specifies an action to be performed when the field receives focus.
onchange	For use with scripts. An event handle that specifies an action to be performed when the content of the field has been changed.
onblur	For use with scripts. An event handle that specifies an action to be performed when the focus is removed from a field.

Figure 7.11 `<select>` Input Element Attributes

Figure 7.12 shows examples of a `<select>` drop-down list. Figure 7.13 shows how they look in a browser. Figure 7.14 shows how the drop-down list in the City item looks when the list is clicked. In the example, the Houston option is chosen.

```
1   <h4>Choose which city you live in:</h4>
2   <select name="state" size="1">
3       <option value="boston">Boston</option>
4       <option value="chicago">Chicago</option>
5       <option value="cincinnati">Cincinnati</option>
6       <option value="dallas">Dallas</option>
7       <option value="detroit">Detroit</option>
8       <option value="houston">Houston</option>
9       <option value="los angeles">Los Angeles</option>
10      <option value="new york">New York</option>
11      <option value="richmond">Richmond</option>
12      <option value="washington">Washington DC</option>
13  </select>
```

```
1   <h4>Choose which cities you have visited (can choose
        more than one):</h4>
2   <select name="visited" size="3" multiple="multiple">
3       <option value="boston">Boston</option>
4       <option value="chicago">Chicago</option>
5       <option value="cincinnati">Cincinnati</option>
6       <option value="dallas">Dallas</option>
7       <option value="detroit">Detroit</option>
8       <option value="houston">Houston</option>
9       <option value="los angeles">Los Angeles</option>
10      <option value="new york">New York</option>
11      <option value="richmond">Richmond</option>
12      <option value="washington">Washington DC</option>
13  </select>
```

Figure 7.12 `<select>` Input Element Examples

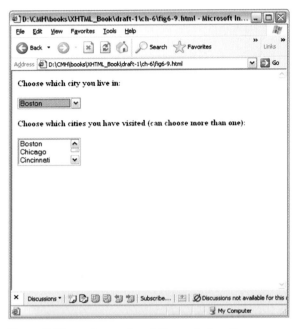

Figure 7.13 `<select>` Input Elements in a Browser

Figure 7.14 `<select>` Input Elements in a Browser with Drop-Down List for "Houston" Selected

Submitting and Clearing the Form

Once a user has completed the form, the data must be sent to the server. In addition to this functionality, most forms also contain functionality that will allow the user to clear or reset the form fields. The actions of submitting and clearing the form elements are fundamental to XHTML forms. These two elements appear as buttons on the Web page which the user can click to either submit the form to the server using the `submit` option, or to reset the form back to the default values using the `reset` option. They are specified in the `<input />` element by the `type` attribute:

```
<input type="submit" />
<input type="reset" />
```

The `value` attribute can be set to assign names to these buttons. This text will show up on the button. If no value is set for `value`, then the computer will assign default text to the buttons. Figure 7.15 shows examples of "Submit" and "Reset" buttons and Figure 7.16 shows how they look in a browser.

```
1    <input type="submit" /><br />
2    <input type="reset" /><br />
3    <input type="submit" value="Submit this form" /><br />
4    <input type="reset" value="Clear the form values" /><br />
```

Figure 7.15 Submit and Reset Input Element Examples

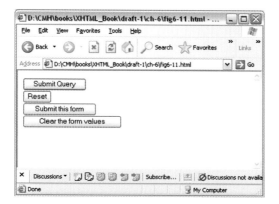

Figure 7.16 Submit and Reset Input Elements in a Browser

Form Elements

◎◎ Form Example

Let's build an XHTML form that uses the elements that we've covered in this chapter. The XHTML document in Figure 7.17 shows the code for our Web page that contains a form. The form elements have been highlighted in red. Figure 7.18 shows our form in a browser.

```
1    <?xml version="1.0"?>
2    <!DOCTYPE html PUBLIC "-//W3C//DTD XHTML 1.0 Strict//EN"
3        "http://www.w3.org/TR/xhtml1/DTD/xhtml1-strict.dtd">
4    <html xmlns="http://www.w3.org/1999/xhtml">
5        <head>
6            <title>Account Application</title>
7        </head>
8        <body>
9            <div>
10               <h1>Account Application</h1>
11               <hr />
12           </div>
13           <form action="/cgi-bin/process.cgi" method="get">
14               <p>
15                   Please enter your name:
                     <input type="text" name="name" size="35" />
16               </p>
17               <p>
18                   Enter your password:
                     <input type="password" name="pw" size="35"   />
19               </p>
20               <p>
21                   Enter your password again to verify: <input
                     type="password" name="password2" size="35"   />
22               </p>
23               <p>
24                   Please select the accounts you currently have:<br />
25                   <input type="checkbox" name="accounts" value="101" />
                         Checking<br />
26                   <input type="checkbox" name="accounts" value="102" />
                         Savings<br />
27                   <input type="checkbox" name="accounts" value=103" />
                         Brokerage<br />
28                   <input type="checkbox" name="accounts" value="104" />
                         Retirement<br />
```

```
29              </p>
30              <p>
31                 Are you employed?<br />
32                 <input type="radio" name="emp" value="yes"
                       checked="checked" />Yes<br />
33                 <input type="radio" name="emp" value="no" />No<br />
34              </p>
35              <h4>Choose the branch office closest to where you live:
                </h4>
36              <p>
37                 <select name="branch" size="1">
38                 <option value="braintree">Braintree</option>
39                 <option value="cambridge">Cambridge</option>
40                 <option value="dedham">Dedham</option>
41                 <option value="foxboro">Foxboro</option>
42                 <option value="hingham">Hingham</option>
43                 <option value="marlborough">Marlborough</option>
44                 <option value="weymouth">Weymouth</option>
45                 </select>
46              </p>
47              <p>Please provide any additional information:<br />
48                 <textarea name="example1" rows="7"
                   cols="35"></textarea>
49              </p>
50              <p>
52                 <input type="submit" value="Submit Application" />
53                 <input type="reset" value="Reset Form" /><br />
54              </p>
55          </form>
56      </body>
57  </html>
```

Figure 7.17 XHTML Document for Form Example

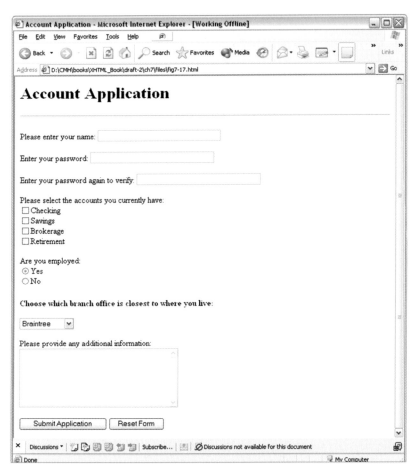

Figure 7.18 Form Example in a Browser

☆ Summary

▷ Web forms have been a part of XHTML and HTML standards for many years.

▷ Most Web browsers and other Web clients are capable of using forms.

▷ All form elements are contained within the `<form>` element.

▷ The data submitted on forms is sent to a program on the server that processes the data.

▷ The three types of text input elements are text, password, and file.

▷ The `<textarea>` element provides a large text input box for data.

▷ The three types of selection elements are checkbox, radio, and select.

▷ Checkboxes allow users to select multiple items, while radio buttons only allow one selection.

▷ The "Submit" and "Reset" buttons are commonly used on forms to submit the form data and reset the form, respectively.

☆ Online References

W3 School's HTML forms tutorial
`http://www.w3schools.com/html/html_forms.asp`

Webmonkey's HTML forms
`http://hotwired.lycos.com/webmonkey/99/30/index4a.html?tw=authoring`

The Extensible Stylesheet Language (XSL)
`http://www.w3.org/Style/XSL/`

W3 School's JavaScript tutorial
`http://www.w3schools.com/js/default.asp`

W3 School's XHTML form element
`http://www.w3schools.com/tags/tag_form.asp`

W3 School's XHTML input element
`http://www.w3schools.com/tags/tag_input.asp`

W3 School's XHTML text area element
`http://www.w3schools.com/tags/tag_textarea.asp`

W3 School's XHTML select elements
`http://www.w3schools.com/tags/tag_select.asp`

MIT's cgiemail Web form email script homepage
`http://web.mit.edu/wwwdev/cgiemail/`

☆ Review Questions

1. What are three uses of Web forms?
2. What are the two methods that can be used to send data to the server and what is the difference between them?
3. Of the two methods from Question 2, which is the default method?
4. What is the only required attribute for the `<form>` element?
5. Which element replaces the user text with asterisks?
6. Which two attributes for the `<textarea>` element control the size of the area?
7. Which selection element allows a user to check multiple boxes?
8. How do you enable multiple selections for the `<select>` element?
9. What does the `reset` option do?

☆ Hands-On Exercises

1. Write the beginning `<form>` element tag to send the form data to a program on the same server, /cgi-bin/form.cgi, that uses the `post` method. Using this `<form>` start tag, create an XHTML document containing a form that asks for a user's name (text input element) and password (password input element). Test your results in the W3C Validator.

2. Add a drop-down list named Age that contains the numbers 21 through 35 to indicate the age of the user filling out the form. Make sure you allow the user to select only one entry.

3. Create a checkbox group named Classes for the following list of courses. Use the Course ID as the value for each checkbox.

   Course ID: EN 1101
   Course Name: Introduction to Shakespeare

   Course ID: CS 2119
   Course Name: Advanced Computer Networking

   Course ID: PH 5428
   Course Name: History of Philosophy

   Course ID: MT 8759
   Course Name: Statistical Analysis

4. Create a radio button group for the courses in Exercise 3, making course EN 1101 the default selected course.

5. Starting with the document you created in Exercise 1, use a style sheet to create the layout shown on the facing page.

WHAT'S NEXT?

T his chapter will introduce you to new technologies related to XHTML. Some of these technologies are not yet widely supported. Here you will find an overview of what's currently being developed and what's in the future with XHTML.

Chapter Objectives

☆ Discuss the future of XHTML technologies

☆ Describe module-based XHTML

☆ Understand XForms and XHTML-Print modules

☆ Discover the next versions of XHTML: XHTML 1.1 and XHTML 2.0

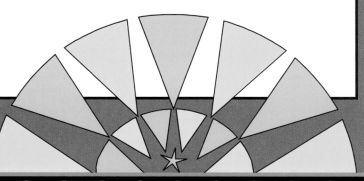

◎◎ The Future of XHTML

XHTML is poised for the future of Web development, and many new technologies are being developed around the XHTML 1.0 standards that you've learned about in this book. The Web community is rapidly accepting XHTML as a replacement to HTML because of its compatibility with existing browsers and to new XML technologies and standards. This chapter describes some of the new technologies being developed around and in addition to XHTML. You've already read about one new technology, XFrames, in Chapter Six. Keep in mind that many of these technologies are very new and are not yet supported in many browsers.

XHTML is positioned to become modularized, and to very clearly separate presentation from document content and structure. We've already seen the beginnings of this in the XHTML Strict version of XHTML 1.0, where many of the strictly presentational HTML elements have been excluded in favor of style sheets. In a few years, XHTML will not be simply one language, but a set of languages and specifications that interact with each other. As a document author or developer, you will have a suite of tools at your disposal for creating different types of content. You will start with a base language that gives you limited features and functionality, then you will be able to plug in other modules as needed, depending on the type of document you are working with. For example, future releases of XHTML will more than likely *not* contain support for forms by default. Developers will use the base language to develop the document, then include the XHTML forms module, XForms, in order to include a form on the page.

This chapter briefly introduces you to XHTML-related technologies that have been or are being developed at this writing. Links where you can find more information are provided at the end of the chapter.

◎◎ XHTML Basic

The **XHTML Basic** specification was released as a recommendation by the W3C in December of 2000. XHTML Basic was developed for use with small client devices that do not have the processing power for the full element set of XHTML. XHTML Basic contains a subset of XHTML elements, including basic text formatting (headings, paragraphs, lists, etc.), hyperlinks, images, basic forms, and tables. The base set of elements for XHTML Basic is limited, but it can be extended if needed.

XHTML Basic documents must conform to the same general guidelines as other XML-based documents as far as syntax is concerned. It has, however, its own DTD that must be referenced. Following is the DTD declaration for an XHTML document:

```
<!DOCTYPE html PUBLIC "-//W3C//DTD XHTML Basic 1.0//EN"
    "http://www.w3.org/TR/xhtml-basic/xhtml-basic10.dtd">
```

According to the W3C, the following are client devices that could benefit from this smaller language:

☆ Mobile phones

☆ Televisions

☆ PDAs

☆ Vending machines

☆ Pagers

☆ Car navigation systems

☆ Mobile game machines

☆ Digital book readers

☆ Smart watches

☻☺ Modularization of XHTML

The **Modularization of XHTML** specification was released as a recommendation in April of 2001. XHTML Modularization is probably the most radical deviation from traditional HTML since its inception. The idea behind modularization is to reorganize the XHTML markup language by functionality.

This is a huge change from the traditional structure of HTML because one of the strong points of HTML has always been its compact size and ease of use. Having all of the HTML elements in the same DTD made the language very easy to use. However, it also made it very static and almost impossible to extend if needed. This need for extendibility has finally overridden the convenience of the small structure. Future versions of XHTML will not contain the entire XHTML element set. There will be one XHTML DTD that contains the base element set for page structure, and a collection of other DTDs, or **modules**, that contain the element sets for various pieces of functionality. We are seeing this already with the development of XForms, XFrames, and XHTML Basic.

The W3C describes modularization as follows:

> The architecture of XHTML's modularization is simple: a basic framework of XHTML modules enables the development of XHTML-conforming markup languages. These new languages must use the basic framework, and may also use other XHTML-provided modules, other W3C-defined modules, or indeed any other module that is correctly defined. The modules plug together within the XHTML framework to define a markup language that is task or client specific, but which is based upon the familiar (X)HTML structure. This new markup language is appropriate for a development of portable, XHTML-conforming content. Documents developed against this new markup language will be usable on any XHTML-conforming clients. In many cases, the content will also be portable to existing HTML 4 browsers.

◎◎ XHTML 1.1–Module-Based XHTML

The **XHTML 1.1—module-based XHTML** specification was released as a recommendation by the W3C in May 2001. XHTML 1.1 is the base language for module-based XHTML. It is meant to serve as a base language that can be extended by other XHTML document types. Like XHTML 1.0, the XHTML 1.1 element set will be compatible with current browsers. However, XHTML 1.1 does not support many of the presentational elements that we have discussed throughout this book, and is built on XHTML Strict. XHTML 1.1 will rely solely on style sheets for presentational information.

XHTML 1.1 documents must conform to the same standards for well-formed documents as XHTML 1.0 documents. According to the W3C, the strategy behind XHTML 1.1 is to provide a markup language that is rich in structural features and functionality, but that relies on style sheets for its presentational data. One of the most important changes between XHTML 1.0 and XHTML 1.1 is that on the `<a>` and `<map>` elements, the `name` attribute has been removed in favor of the `id` attribute.

XHTML 1.1, like other versions, has its own DTD declaration. Figure 8.1 shows a minimal XHTML 1.1 document, with the XHTML 1.1 DTD declaration on line 3.

```
1    <?xml version="1.0" encoding="UTF-8"?>
2    <!DOCTYPE html PUBLIC "-//W3C//DTD XHTML 1.1//EN"
3       "http://www.w3.org/TR/xhtml11/DTD/xhtml11.dtd">
4    <html xmlns="http://www.w3.org/1999/xhtml" xml:lang="en">
5       <head>
6          <title>XHTML 1.1 Document</title>
7       </head>
8       <body>
9          <p>XHTML 1.1 is based on module-based XHTML.</p>
10      </body>
11   </html>
```

Figure 8.1 XHTML 1.1 Sample Document

◎◎ XHTML 2.0

The **XHTML 2.0** specification is not yet a released recommendation. It is currently in draft form. Draft 6 was released in May of 2003. XHTML 2.0, the largest break from traditional HTML and XHTML yet, is comprised of a number of XHTML modules that describe the elements and attributes of the language. Many of the modules in XHTML 2.0 are updates and/or extensions to the modules defined in the Modularization of XHTML 1.0 specification.

XHTML 2.0 takes a bold step away from backward-compatibility with older browsers and relies more heavily on newer browsers with extensive support for XML languages. For example, elements for frames and forms have been replaced, and the <img> element is gone. XHTML 2.0 relies on XForms and XFrames for the functionality previously provided by XHTML form and frame elements.

Many other familiar elements, like <br /> and the heading elements, <h1> through <h6>, are being deprecated in favor of more structural elements, like <line> and <section>. Because this specification is still in draft form, we don't know exactly what will be included or excluded. Following are the design aims, from the W3C Web site, for developing XHTML 2.0:

☆ As generic XML as possible: If a facility exists in XML, try to use that rather than duplicating it.

☆ Less presentation, more structure.

☆ More usability: Try to make the language easy to write, and make the resulting documents easy to use.

☆ More accessibility: Some call it "designing for our future selves"; the design should be as inclusive as possible.

☆ Better internationalization: It is a World Wide Web.

☆ More device independence: New devices coming online, such as telephones, PDAs, tablets, televisions, and so on, means that user must be allowed to author once and render in different ways on different devices, rather than authoring new versions of the document for each type of device.

☆ Less scripting: Achieving functionality through scripting is difficult for the author and restricts the type of agent that can be used to view the document. We have tried to identify current typical usage, and include those usages in markup.

This specification is not yet complete, so keep an eye on the W3C Web site for updates about XHTML 2.0.

◎◎ XHTML-Print

The **XHTML-Print** specification is very close to becoming a recommendation. In January of 2004, XHTML-Print became a W3C candidate recommendation, one of the last steps in the process. XHTML is part of the modularization of the XHTML family and is being designed for printing from mobile devices.

XHTML-Print is based on XHTML Basic and CSS. According to the W3C, "its targeted usage is for printing in environments where it is not feasible or desirable to install a printer-specific driver and where some variability in the formatting of the output is acceptable." Because XHTML-Print aims to be simple, complex page layouts will not be possible. For example, XHTML-Print allows only portrait page layout, and the page prints from top to bottom and left to right. One of the primary benefits of XHTML-Print is that it will not require a printer-specific driver to be installed on the printer in order to print properly.

XForms

The **XForms** specification is a new technology being developed by the W3C and is not yet a recommendation. The latest proposed recommendation was released in August of 2003. In January 2004 the W3C released its requirements for XForms 1.1. The W3C describes the XForms recommendation as follows:

> *XForms is an XML application that represents the next generation of forms for the Web. By splitting traditional XHTML forms into three parts—XForms model, instance data, and user interface—it separates presentation from content, allows reuse, and gives strong typing, thereby reducing the number of round-trips to the server, as well as offering device independence and a reduced need for scripting. XForms is not a free-standing document type, but is intended to be integrated into other markup languages, such as XHTML.*

XForms will more than likely replace the form elements in the current HTML and XHTML specifications. Unlike current forms, XForms will be useable with a wide variety of platforms, including desktop computers, handheld PDAs, information appliances, and even paper. It is being developed to work with any XML language, not just XHTML.

XForms is an excellent example of how modularization works. Figure 8.2 is an image from the W3C Web site that shows how the XForms module can be added to a wide variety of other XML-based technologies.

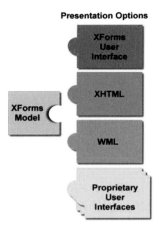

Figure 8.2 XForms Module

☆ Summary

▷ XHTML Basic is primarily used with clients that have limited resources, like phones and PDAs.

▷ XHTML modularization is a new standard reorganizing XHTML into functional element sets.

▷ XHTML 1.1 and XHTML 2.0 are the new versions of XHTML being developed as successors to XHTML 1.0.

▷ XFrames and XForms are two functional element sets that are part of the XHTML modularization initiative.

▷ XHTML-Print is being developed to allow XHTML-enabled devices to print without specific printer drivers being pre-installed on the printers.

☆ Online References

W3C XHTML basic recommendation
`http://www.w3.org/TR/xhtml-basic/`

W3C XHTML 1.1 recommendation
`http://www.w3.org/TR/xhtml11/`

W3C XHTML 2.0 working draft
`http://www.w3.org/TR/xhtml2/`

W3C modularization of XHTML overview
`http://www.w3.org/MarkUp/modularization`

W3C modularization of XHTML recommendation
`http://www.w3.org/TR/xhtml-modularization/`

W3C XFrames working draft
`http://www.w3.org/TR/xframes/`

XHTML-Print W3C candidate recommendation
`http://www.w3.org/TR/2004/CR-xhtml-print-20040120/`

W3C XForms 1.0 proposed recommendation
`http://www.w3.org/TR/xsl`

☆ Review Questions

1. What does it mean to separate presentation from content, and why is this a good idea?

2. XHTML is moving toward a modularized form. Explain the reasoning behind this.

3. Explain why XHTML Basic does not contain the entire element set for XHTML.

4. Give two reasons why XHTML 2.0 is moving away from backward compatibility with existing and older Web browsers.

5. XHTML-Print is being developed primarily for what types of devices?

6. What is the biggest strength of the new XForms technology?

☆ Hands-On Exercises

1. What is the DOCTYPE declaration for XHTML 2.0?

2. Research XHTML-Print on the W3C Web site and list three XHTML modules it supports. The structure and text modules are two examples.

3. What are the differences between XHTML 1.0, XHTML 1.1, XHTML 2.0, and XHTML Basic?

4. Research and provide a brief description of the modularization of XHTML in XML schema working draft.

5. Describe how the XForms module can be used with XML languages and technologies.

APPENDIX A: XHTML DTDS

The Document Type Definitions (DTDs) for each of the three versions of XHTML define the rules for the language. DTDs are part of the XML family of technologies, are used to describe the details of XML document types, and can be found on the W3C Web site, www.w3c.org.

> ☆ **TIP**
>
> The Internet location of the DTD documents is listed in the DOCTYPE declaration for each version of XHTML:
>
> **Transitional:** `http://www.w3.org/TR/xhtml1/DTD/xhtml1-transitional.dtd`
>
> **Frameset:** `http://www.w3.org/TR/xhtml1/DTD/xhtml1-frameset.dtd`
>
> **Strict:** `http://www.w3.org/TR/xhtml1/DTD/xhtml1-strict.dtd`

DTDs may seem a bit intimidating at first, but you will find that they are invaluable reference documents once you learn how to read them. They contain the list of the valid element and attribute names that can be used with each XHTML document type. For each element, the DTD specifies which other elements, if any, are required to be contained within the element. It also specifies which attributes are allowed for the element, and if any of those attributes are required.

Following is the syntax for an element:

```
1    <!ELEMENT    element_name   (content model)>
2    <!ATTLIST element_name
3        attribute_name-1        datatype        default_value
4        attribute_name-2        datatype        default_value
5        ...
6        attribute_name-n        datatype        default_value >
```

Line 1 defines the element name and the *content model* for the element. The *content model* for an element simply defines what type of information the element can contain, such as content or other elements. Line 2 begins the declaration for the attributes that are allowed for this element. An element can have zero or many attributes defined. The attribute names, datatypes, and default values are defined on lines 3 through 6. The *datatype* of the attribute describes what kind of data it can contain, and the *default value* tells you whether that attribute is required or not, and whether there is a default value assigned if it is not specified in the document itself. Following are the three possible default value types for attributes:

1. FIXED—The value for the attribute is fixed. The value of the attribute must match the value assigned in the DTD.

2. REQUIRED—This attribute is required. The element must contain this attribute, and it must have a value to be valid.

3. IMPLIED—This attribute is optional. The element may or may not contain this attribute. It can be omitted and still be valid.

Let's look at an example of a DTD definition for an element. Following are the DTD definitions for the <html> element for each of the XML document types.

Transitional and Strict

```
1 <!ELEMENT html (head, body)>
2 <!ATTLIST html
3    %i18n;
4    id            ID              #IMPLIED
5    xmlns         %URI;           #FIXED
     'http://www.w3.org/1999/xhtml'>
```

Frameset

```
1 <!ELEMENT html (head, frameset)>
2 <!ATTLIST html
3    %i18n;
4    id            ID              #IMPLIED
5    xmlns         %URI;           #FIXED
     'http://www.w3.org/1999/xhtml'>
```

In both definitions, line 1 defines the element name, <html>. The content model defines the type of data that can be contained within the start and end tags for this element. In the case of Transitional and Strict, the head and body elements are the only valid elements that can be inside the <html> element. For Frameset, the <body> element is replaced with the <frameset> element. Line 2 starts the attribute list for the <html> element. Line 3, %i18n; pertains to internationalization for different languages. Lines 4 and 5 define the attributes that are valid for this element. On line 4, the id attribute's datatype is ID, which means the value of this attribute must be a unique identifier. Its default value is set to IMPLIED, which means this attribute is optional. The attribute on line 5, xmlns, has a datatype of URI, meaning that the value of this attribute must be a Uniform Resource Identifier. The xmlns attribute defines the XML Namespace (see Chapter 3) that this document uses. In the case of this attribute, its value is FIXED, meaning that it is required and cannot be changed or overridden in the document. Attributes that are FIXED are not required to be written in the start tag of the element, but will be added automatically by applications that parse the document.

You will find entries like the ones above for every XHTML element in the DTDs. There is a lot of other information contained in the DTDs that is beyond the scope of this book. The Web site for the W3C is a good starting point for more information.

XHTML Strict DTD

```
<!--
    Extensible HTML version 1.0 Strict DTD

    This is the same as HTML 4 Strict except for
    changes due to the differences between XML and SGML.

    Namespace = http://www.w3.org/1999/xhtml

    For further information, see:
       http://www.w3.org/TR/xhtml1

    Copyright (c) 1998-2002 W3C (MIT, INRIA, Keio),
    All Rights Reserved.

    This DTD module is identified by the PUBLIC and SYSTEM
       identifiers:

    PUBLIC "-//W3C//DTD XHTML 1.0 Strict//EN"
    SYSTEM "http://www.w3.org/TR/xhtml1/DTD/
       xhtml1-strict.dtd"

    $Revision: 1.1 $
    $Date: 2002/08/01 13:56:03 $

-->

<!--================= Character mnemonic entities
=========================-->

<!ENTITY % HTMLlat1 PUBLIC
    "-//W3C//ENTITIES Latin 1 for XHTML//EN"
    "xhtml-lat1.ent">
%HTMLlat1;

<!ENTITY % HTMLsymbol PUBLIC
    "-//W3C//ENTITIES Symbols for XHTML//EN"
    "xhtml-symbol.ent">
%HTMLsymbol;

<!ENTITY % HTMLspecial PUBLIC
    "-//W3C//ENTITIES Special for XHTML//EN"
    "xhtml-special.ent">
%HTMLspecial;
```

```
<!--================ Imported Names ====================-->

<!ENTITY % ContentType "CDATA">
    <!-- media type, as per [RFC2045] -->

<!ENTITY % ContentTypes "CDATA">
    <!-- comma-separated list of media types, as per
    [RFC2045] -->

<!ENTITY % Charset "CDATA">
    <!-- a character encoding, as per [RFC2045] -->

<!ENTITY % Charsets "CDATA">
    <!-- a space separated list of character encodings, as
    per [RFC2045] -->

<!ENTITY % LanguageCode "NMTOKEN">
    <!-- a language code, as per [RFC3066] -->

<!ENTITY % Character "CDATA">
    <!-- a single character, as per section 2.2 of [XML] -->

<!ENTITY % Number "CDATA">
    <!-- one or more digits -->

<!ENTITY % LinkTypes "CDATA">
    <!-- space-separated list of link types -->

<!ENTITY % MediaDesc "CDATA">
    <!-- single or comma-separated list of media
    descriptors -->

<!ENTITY % URI "CDATA">
    <!-- a Uniform Resource Identifier, see [RFC2396] -->

<!ENTITY % UriList "CDATA">
    <!-- a space separated list of Uniform Resource
    Identifiers -->

<!ENTITY % Datetime "CDATA">
    <!-- date and time information. ISO date format -->

<!ENTITY % Script "CDATA">
    <!-- script expression -->

<!ENTITY % StyleSheet "CDATA">
    <!-- style sheet data -->
```

```
<!ENTITY % Text "CDATA">
    <!-- used for titles etc. -->

<!ENTITY % Length "CDATA">
    <!-- nn for pixels or nn% for percentage length -->

<!ENTITY % MultiLength "CDATA">
    <!-- pixel, percentage, or relative -->

<!ENTITY % Pixels "CDATA">
    <!-- integer representing length in pixels -->

<!-- these are used for image maps -->

<!ENTITY % Shape "(rect|circle|poly|default)">

<!ENTITY % Coords "CDATA">
    <!-- comma separated list of lengths -->

<!--================ Generic Attributes ===================-->

<!-- core attributes common to most elements
  id          document-wide unique id
  class       space separated list of classes
  style       associated style info
  title       advisory title/amplification
-->
<!ENTITY % coreattrs
 "id          ID                      #IMPLIED
  class       CDATA                   #IMPLIED
  style       %StyleSheet;            #IMPLIED
  title       %Text;                  #IMPLIED"
  >

<!-- internationalization attributes
  lang        language code (backwards compatible)
  xml:lang    language code (as per XML 1.0 spec)
  dir         direction for weak/neutral text
-->
<!ENTITY % i18n
 "lang        %LanguageCode;          #IMPLIED
  xml:lang    %LanguageCode;          #IMPLIED
  dir         (ltr|rtl)               #IMPLIED"
  >
```

```
<!-- attributes for common UI events
  onclick         a pointer button was clicked
  ondblclick      a pointer button was double clicked
  onmousedown     a pointer button was pressed down
  onmouseup       a pointer button was released
  onmousemove     a pointer was moved onto the element
  onmouseout      a pointer was moved away from the element
  onkeypress      a key was pressed and released
  onkeydown       a key was pressed down
  onkeyup         a key was released
-->
<!ENTITY % events
 "onclick         %Script;        #IMPLIED
  ondblclick      %Script;        #IMPLIED
  onmousedown     %Script;        #IMPLIED
  onmouseup       %Script;        #IMPLIED
  onmouseover     %Script;        #IMPLIED
  onmousemove     %Script;        #IMPLIED
  onmouseout      %Script;        #IMPLIED
  onkeypress      %Script;        #IMPLIED
  onkeydown       %Script;        #IMPLIED
  onkeyup         %Script;        #IMPLIED"
  >

<!-- attributes for elements that can get the focus
  accesskey       accessibility key character
  tabindex        position in tabbing order
  onfocus         the element got the focus
  onblur          the element lost the focus
-->
<!ENTITY % focus
 "accesskey       %Character;     #IMPLIED
  tabindex        %Number;        #IMPLIED
  onfocus         %Script;        #IMPLIED
  onblur          %Script;        #IMPLIED"
  >

<!ENTITY % attrs "%coreattrs; %i18n; %events;">

<!--=============== Text Elements =====================-->

<!ENTITY % special.pre
    "br | span | bdo | map">

<!ENTITY % special
    "%special.pre; | object | img ">
```

```
<!ENTITY % fontstyle "tt | i | b | big | small ">

<!ENTITY % phrase "em | strong | dfn | code | q |
        samp | kbd | var | cite | abbr | acronym |
        sub | sup ">

<!ENTITY % inline.forms "input | select | textarea |
        label | button">

<!-- these can occur at block or inline level -->
<!ENTITY % misc.inline "ins | del | script">

<!-- these can only occur at block level -->
<!ENTITY % misc "noscript | %misc.inline;">

<!ENTITY % inline "a | %special; | %fontstyle; | %phrase; |
        %inline.forms;">

<!-- %Inline; covers inline or "text-level" elements -->
<!ENTITY % Inline "(#PCDATA | %inline; | %misc.inline;)*">

<!--=============== Block level elements ==================-->

<!ENTITY % heading "h1|h2|h3|h4|h5|h6">
<!ENTITY % lists "ul | ol | dl">
<!ENTITY % blocktext "pre | hr | blockquote | address">

<!ENTITY % block
        "p | %heading; | div | %lists; | %blocktext; |
        fieldset | table">

<!ENTITY % Block "(%block; | form | %misc;)*">

<!-- %Flow; mixes block and inline and is used for list
          items etc. -->
<!ENTITY % Flow "(#PCDATA | %block; | form | %inline; |
        %misc;)*">

<!--=========== Content models for exclusions ===========-->

<!-- a elements use %Inline; excluding a -->

<!ENTITY % a.content
        "(#PCDATA | %special; | %fontstyle; | %phrase; |
        %inline.forms; | %misc.inline;)*">
```

```
<!-- pre uses %Inline excluding big, small, sup or sup -->

<!ENTITY % pre.content
   "(#PCDATA | a | %fontstyle; | %phrase; | %special.pre; |
   %misc.inline;
       | %inline.forms;)*">

<!-- form uses %Block; excluding form -->

<!ENTITY % form.content "(%block; | %misc;)*">

<!-- button uses %Flow; but excludes a, form and form
controls -->

<!ENTITY % button.content
   "(#PCDATA | p | %heading; | div | %lists; | %blocktext;
   | table | %special; | %fontstyle; | %phrase; |
   %misc;)*">

<!--=============== Document Structure ===================-->

<!-- the namespace URI designates the document profile -->

<!ELEMENT html (head, body)>
<!ATTLIST html
  %i18n;
  id             ID              #IMPLIED
  xmlns          %URI;           #FIXED
  'http://www.w3.org/1999/xhtml'
  >

<!--================== Document Head =====================-->

<!ENTITY % head.misc "(script|style|meta|link|object)*">

<!-- content model is %head.misc; combined with a single
     title and an optional base element in any order -->

<!ELEMENT head (%head.misc;,
     ((title, %head.misc;, (base, %head.misc;)?) |
      (base, %head.misc;, (title, %head.misc;))))>

<!ATTLIST head
  %i18n;
  id             ID              #IMPLIED
  profile        %URI;           #IMPLIED
  >
```

```
<!-- The title element is not considered part of the flow
of text. It should be displayed, for example as the page
header or window title. Exactly one title is required per
document.
    -->
<!ELEMENT title (#PCDATA)>
<!ATTLIST title
  %i18n;
  id               ID              #IMPLIED
  >


<!-- document base URI -->

<!ELEMENT base EMPTY>
<!ATTLIST base
  href             %URI;           #REQUIRED
  id               ID              #IMPLIED
  >


<!-- generic metainformation -->
<!ELEMENT meta EMPTY>
<!ATTLIST meta
  %i18n;
  id               ID              #IMPLIED
  http-equiv       CDATA           #IMPLIED
  name             CDATA           #IMPLIED
  content          CDATA           #REQUIRED
  scheme           CDATA           #IMPLIED
  >


<!--
  Relationship values can be used in principle:

    a) for document specific toolbars/menus when used
       with the link element in document head e.g.
         start, contents, previous, next, index, end, help
    b) to link to a separate style sheet (rel="stylesheet")
    c) to make a link to a script (rel="script")
    d) by stylesheets to control how collections of
       html nodes are rendered into printed documents
    e) to make a link to a printable version of this
       document e.g. a PostScript or PDF version
       (rel="alternate" media="print")
  -->
```

```
<!ELEMENT link EMPTY>
<!ATTLIST link
  %attrs;
  charset        %Charset;           #IMPLIED
  href           %URI;               #IMPLIED
  hreflang       %LanguageCode;      #IMPLIED
  type           %ContentType;       #IMPLIED
  rel            %LinkTypes;         #IMPLIED
  rev            %LinkTypes;         #IMPLIED
  media          %MediaDesc;         #IMPLIED
  >

<!-- style info, which may include CDATA sections -->
<!ELEMENT style (#PCDATA)>
<!ATTLIST style
  %i18n;
  id             ID                  #IMPLIED
  type           %ContentType;       #REQUIRED
  media          %MediaDesc;         #IMPLIED
  title          %Text;              #IMPLIED
  xml:space      (preserve)          #FIXED 'preserve'
  >

<!-- script statements, which may include CDATA sections -->
<!ELEMENT script (#PCDATA)>
<!ATTLIST script
  id             ID                  #IMPLIED
  charset        %Charset;           #IMPLIED
  type           %ContentType;       #REQUIRED
  src            %URI;               #IMPLIED
  defer          (defer)             #IMPLIED
  xml:space      (preserve)          #FIXED 'preserve'
  >

<!-- alternate content container for non script-based
rendering -->

<!ELEMENT noscript %Block;>
<!ATTLIST noscript
  %attrs;
  >
```

```
<!--================ Document Body ====================-->

<!ELEMENT body %Block;>
<!ATTLIST body
  %attrs;
  onload              %Script;          #IMPLIED
  onunload            %Script;          #IMPLIED
  >

<!ELEMENT div %Flow;>   <!-- generic language/style
    container -->
<!ATTLIST div
  %attrs;
  >


<!--=================== Paragraphs ====================-->

<!ELEMENT p %Inline;>
<!ATTLIST p
  %attrs;
  >


<!--==================== Headings =====================-->

<!--
   There are six levels of headings from h1 (the most
   important) to h6 (the least important).
-->

<!ELEMENT h1   %Inline;>
<!ATTLIST h1
    %attrs;
    >

<!ELEMENT h2 %Inline;>
<!ATTLIST h2
    %attrs;
    >

<!ELEMENT h3 %Inline;>
<!ATTLIST h3
    %attrs;
    >
```

```
<!ELEMENT h4 %Inline;>
<!ATTLIST h4
   %attrs;
   >

<!ELEMENT h5 %Inline;>
<!ATTLIST h5
   %attrs;
   >

<!ELEMENT h6 %Inline;>
<!ATTLIST h6
   %attrs;
   >

<!--==================== Lists =========================-->

<!-- Unordered list -->

<!ELEMENT ul (li)+>
<!ATTLIST ul
  %attrs;
  >

<!-- Ordered (numbered) list -->

<!ELEMENT ol (li)+>
<!ATTLIST ol
  %attrs;
  >

<!-- list item -->

<!ELEMENT li %Flow;>
<!ATTLIST li
  %attrs;
  >

<!-- definition lists - dt for term, dd for its definition
-->

<!ELEMENT dl (dt|dd)+>
<!ATTLIST dl
  %attrs;
  >
```

```
<!ELEMENT dt %Inline;>
<!ATTLIST dt
  %attrs;
  >

<!ELEMENT dd %Flow;>
<!ATTLIST dd
  %attrs;
  >

<!--==================== Address ======================-->

<!-- information on author -->

<!ELEMENT address %Inline;>
<!ATTLIST address
  %attrs;
  >

<!--================= Horizontal Rule =================-->

<!ELEMENT hr EMPTY>
<!ATTLIST hr
  %attrs;
  >

<!--=============== Preformatted Text ================-->

<!-- content is %Inline; excluding
"img|object|big|small|sub|sup" -->

<!ELEMENT pre %pre.content;>
<!ATTLIST pre
  %attrs;
  xml:space (preserve) #FIXED 'preserve'
  >

<!--================ Block-like Quotes ===============-->

<!ELEMENT blockquote %Block;>
<!ATTLIST blockquote
  %attrs;
  cite          %URI;              #IMPLIED
  >
```

```
<!--============= Inserted/Deleted Text ================-->

<!--
  ins/del are allowed in block and inline content, but its
  inappropriate to include block content within an ins
  element occurring in inline content.
-->
<!ELEMENT ins %Flow;>
<!ATTLIST ins
  %attrs;
  cite           %URI;             #IMPLIED
  datetime       %Datetime;        #IMPLIED
  >

<!ELEMENT del %Flow;>
<!ATTLIST del
  %attrs;
  cite           %URI;             #IMPLIED
  datetime       %Datetime;        #IMPLIED
  >

<!--============= The Anchor Element ================-->

<!-- content is %Inline; except that anchors shouldn't be
nested -->

<!ELEMENT a %a.content;>
<!ATTLIST a
  %attrs;
  %focus;
  charset        %Charset;         #IMPLIED
  type           %ContentType;     #IMPLIED
  name           NMTOKEN           #IMPLIED
  href           %URI;             #IMPLIED
  hreflang       %LanguageCode;    #IMPLIED
  rel            %LinkTypes;       #IMPLIED
  rev            %LinkTypes;       #IMPLIED
  shape          %Shape;           "rect"
  coords         %Coords;          #IMPLIED
  >
<!--================ Inline Elements ================-->

<!ELEMENT span %Inline;> <!-- generic language/style con-
tainer -->
<!ATTLIST span
  %attrs;
  >
```

```
<!ELEMENT bdo %Inline;>        <!-- I18N BiDi over-ride -->
<!ATTLIST bdo
  %coreattrs;
  %events;
  lang              %LanguageCode;    #IMPLIED
  xml:lang          %LanguageCode;    #IMPLIED
  dir               (ltr|rtl)         #REQUIRED
  >

<!ELEMENT br EMPTY>            <!-- forced line break -->
<!ATTLIST br
  %coreattrs;
  >

<!ELEMENT em %Inline;>        <!-- emphasis -->
<!ATTLIST em %attrs;>

<!ELEMENT strong %Inline;>    <!-- strong emphasis -->
<!ATTLIST strong %attrs;>

<!ELEMENT dfn %Inline;>       <!-- definitional -->
<!ATTLIST dfn %attrs;>

<!ELEMENT code %Inline;>      <!-- program code -->
<!ATTLIST code %attrs;>

<!ELEMENT samp %Inline;>      <!-- sample -->
<!ATTLIST samp %attrs;>

<!ELEMENT kbd %Inline;>  <!-- something user would type -->
<!ATTLIST kbd %attrs;>

<!ELEMENT var %Inline;>       <!-- variable -->
<!ATTLIST var %attrs;>

<!ELEMENT cite %Inline;>      <!-- citation -->
<!ATTLIST cite %attrs;>

<!ELEMENT abbr %Inline;>      <!-- abbreviation -->
<!ATTLIST abbr %attrs;>

<!ELEMENT acronym %Inline;>   <!-- acronym -->
<!ATTLIST acronym %attrs;>

<!ELEMENT q %Inline;>         <!-- inlined quote -->
<!ATTLIST q
  %attrs;
  cite              %URI;             #IMPLIED
  >
```

```
<!ELEMENT sub %Inline;>        <!-- subscript -->
<!ATTLIST sub %attrs;>

<!ELEMENT sup %Inline;>        <!-- superscript -->
<!ATTLIST sup %attrs;>

<!ELEMENT tt %Inline;>         <!-- fixed pitch font -->
<!ATTLIST tt %attrs;>

<!ELEMENT i %Inline;>          <!-- italic font -->
<!ATTLIST i %attrs;>

<!ELEMENT b %Inline;>          <!-- bold font -->
<!ATTLIST b %attrs;>

<!ELEMENT big %Inline;>        <!-- bigger font -->
<!ATTLIST big %attrs;>

<!ELEMENT small %Inline;>      <!-- smaller font -->
<!ATTLIST small %attrs;>

<!--===================== Object ========================-->
<!--
    object is used to embed objects as part of HTML pages.
    param elements should precede other content. Parameters
    can also be expressed as attribute/value pairs on the
    object element itself when brevity is desired.
-->

<!ELEMENT object (#PCDATA | param | %block; | form |
%inline; | %misc;)*>
<!ATTLIST object
    %attrs;
    declare         (declare)           #IMPLIED
    classid         %URI;               #IMPLIED
    codebase        %URI;               #IMPLIED
    data            %URI;               #IMPLIED
    type            %ContentType;       #IMPLIED
    codetype        %ContentType;       #IMPLIED
    archive         %UriList;           #IMPLIED
    standby         %Text;              #IMPLIED
    height          %Length;            #IMPLIED
    width           %Length;            #IMPLIED
    usemap          %URI;               #IMPLIED
    name            NMTOKEN             #IMPLIED
    tabindex        %Number;            #IMPLIED
    >
```

```
<!--
   param is used to supply a named property value.
   In XML it would seem natural to follow RDF and support an
   abbreviated syntax where the param elements are replaced
   by attribute value pairs on the object start tag.
-->
<!ELEMENT param EMPTY>
<!ATTLIST param
   id                ID                    #IMPLIED
   name              CDATA                 #IMPLIED
   value             CDATA                 #IMPLIED
   valuetype         (data|ref|object)     "data"
   type              %ContentType;         #IMPLIED
   >


<!--======================= Images =====================-->


<!--
   To avoid accessibility problems for people who aren't
   able to see the image, you should provide a text
   description using the alt and longdesc attributes.
   In addition, avoid the use of server-side image maps.
   Note that in this DTD there is no name attribute. That
   is only available in the transitional and frameset DTD.
-->

<!ELEMENT img EMPTY>
<!ATTLIST img
   %attrs;
   src               %URI;                 #REQUIRED
   alt               %Text;                #REQUIRED
   longdesc          %URI;                 #IMPLIED
   height            %Length;              #IMPLIED
   width             %Length;              #IMPLIED
   usemap            %URI;                 #IMPLIED
   ismap             (ismap)               #IMPLIED
   >

<!-- usemap points to a map element which may be in this
document or an external document, although the latter is
not widely supported -->

<!--============== Client-side image maps =============-->

<!-- These can be placed in the same document or grouped in
a separate document although this isn't yet widely sup-
ported -->
```

```
<!ELEMENT map ((%block; | form | %misc;)+ | area+)>
<!ATTLIST map
  %i18n;
  %events;
  id               ID                    #REQUIRED
  class            CDATA                 #IMPLIED
  style            %StyleSheet;          #IMPLIED
  title            %Text;                #IMPLIED
  name             NMTOKEN               #IMPLIED
  >

<!ELEMENT area EMPTY>
<!ATTLIST area
  %attrs;
  %focus;
  shape            %Shape;               "rect"
  coords           %Coords;              #IMPLIED
  href             %URI;                 #IMPLIED
  nohref           (nohref)              #IMPLIED
  alt              %Text;                #REQUIRED
  >

<!--==================== Forms ========================-->
<!ELEMENT form %form.content;>     <!-- forms shouldn't be
nested -->

<!ATTLIST form
  %attrs;
  action           %URI;                 #REQUIRED
  method           (get|post)            "get"
  enctype          %ContentType;         "application/
                                         x-www-form-urlencoded"
  onsubmit         %Script;              #IMPLIED
  onreset          %Script;              #IMPLIED
  accept           %ContentTypes;        #IMPLIED
  accept-charset %Charsets;              #IMPLIED
  >

<!--
  Each label must not contain more than ONE field
  Label elements shouldn't be nested.
-->
<!ELEMENT label %Inline;>
<!ATTLIST label
  %attrs;
  for              IDREF                 #IMPLIED
  accesskey        %Character;           #IMPLIED
  onfocus          %Script;              #IMPLIED
  onblur           %Script;              #IMPLIED
  >
```

```
<!ENTITY % InputType
  "(text | password | checkbox |
    radio | submit | reset |
    file | hidden | image | button)"
  >

<!-- the name attribute is required for all but submit &
reset -->

<!ELEMENT input EMPTY>        <!-- form control -->
<!ATTLIST input
  %attrs;
  %focus;
  type            %InputType;         "text"
  name            CDATA               #IMPLIED
  value           CDATA               #IMPLIED
  checked         (checked)           #IMPLIED
  disabled        (disabled)          #IMPLIED
  readonly        (readonly)          #IMPLIED
  size            CDATA               #IMPLIED
  maxlength       %Number;            #IMPLIED
  src             %URI;               #IMPLIED
  alt             CDATA               #IMPLIED
  usemap          %URI;               #IMPLIED
  onselect        %Script;            #IMPLIED
  onchange        %Script;            #IMPLIED
  accept          %ContentTypes;      #IMPLIED
  >

<!ELEMENT select (optgroup|option)+>  <!-- option selector
-->
<!ATTLIST select
  %attrs;
  name            CDATA               #IMPLIED
  size            %Number;            #IMPLIED
  multiple        (multiple)          #IMPLIED
  disabled        (disabled)          #IMPLIED
  tabindex        %Number;            #IMPLIED
  onfocus         %Script;            #IMPLIED
  onblur          %Script;            #IMPLIED
  onchange        %Script;            #IMPLIED
  >

<!ELEMENT optgroup (option)+>    <!-- option group -->
<!ATTLIST optgroup
  %attrs;
  disabled        (disabled)          #IMPLIED
  label           %Text;              #REQUIRED
  >
```

```
<!ELEMENT option (#PCDATA)>        <!-- selectable choice -->
<!ATTLIST option
  %attrs;
  selected         (selected)        #IMPLIED
  disabled         (disabled)        #IMPLIED
  label            %Text;            #IMPLIED
  value            CDATA             #IMPLIED
  >


<!ELEMENT textarea (#PCDATA)>        <!-- multi-line text
field -->
<!ATTLIST textarea
  %attrs;
  %focus;
  name             CDATA                  #IMPLIED
  rows             %Number;               #REQUIRED
  cols             %Number;               #REQUIRED
  disabled         (disabled)             #IMPLIED
  readonly         (readonly)             #IMPLIED
  onselect         %Script;               #IMPLIED
  onchange         %Script;               #IMPLIED
  >

<!--
  The fieldset element is used to group form fields.
  Only one legend element should occur in the content
  and if present should only be preceded by whitespace.
-->
<!ELEMENT fieldset (#PCDATA | legend | %block; | form |
%inline; | %misc;)*>
<!ATTLIST fieldset
  %attrs;
  >

<!ELEMENT legend %Inline;>        <!-- fieldset label -->
<!ATTLIST legend
  %attrs;
  accesskey             %Character;             #IMPLIED
  >

<!--
 Content is %Flow; excluding a, form and form controls
-->
```

```
<!ELEMENT button %button.content;>   <!-- push button -->
<!ATTLIST button
  %attrs;
  %focus;
  name            CDATA                    #IMPLIED
  value           CDATA                    #IMPLIED
  type            (button|submit|reset)    "submit"
  disabled        (disabled)               #IMPLIED
  >


<!--===================== Tables =======================-->

<!-- Derived from IETF HTML table standard, see [RFC1942] -->

<!--
The border attribute sets the thickness of the frame around
the table. The default units are screen pixels.

The frame attribute specifies which parts of the frame
around the table should be rendered. The values are not
the same as CALS to avoid a name clash with the valign
attribute.
-->
<!ENTITY % TFrame
"(void|above|below|hsides|lhs|rhs|vsides|box|border)">

<!--
The rules attribute defines which rules to draw between
cells:

If rules is absent then assume: "none" if border is absent
or border="0" otherwise "all"
-->

<!ENTITY % TRules "(none | groups | rows | cols | all)">

<!-- horizontal alignment attributes for cell contents

  char            alignment char, e.g. char=':'
  charoff         offset for alignment char
-->
<!ENTITY % cellhalign
  "align          (left|center|right|justify|char) #IMPLIED
   char           %Character;           #IMPLIED
   charoff        %Length;              #IMPLIED"
  >
```

```
<!-- vertical alignment attributes for cell contents -->
<!ENTITY % cellvalign
    "valign      (top|middle|bottom|baseline) #IMPLIED"
    >

<!ELEMENT table
    (caption?, (col*|colgroup*), thead?, tfoot?,
    (tbody+|tr+))>
<!ELEMENT caption     %Inline;>
<!ELEMENT thead       (tr)+>
<!ELEMENT tfoot       (tr)+>
<!ELEMENT tbody       (tr)+>
<!ELEMENT colgroup    (col)*>
<!ELEMENT col         EMPTY>
<!ELEMENT tr          (th|td)+>
<!ELEMENT th          %Flow;>
<!ELEMENT td          %Flow;>

<!ATTLIST table
    %attrs;
    summary          %Text;        #IMPLIED
    width            %Length;      #IMPLIED
    border           %Pixels;      #IMPLIED
    frame            %TFrame;      #IMPLIED
    rules            %TRules;      #IMPLIED
    cellspacing      %Length;      #IMPLIED
    cellpadding      %Length;      #IMPLIED
    >

<!ATTLIST caption
    %attrs;
    >

<!--
colgroup groups a set of col elements. It allows you to
group several semantically related columns together.
-->
<!ATTLIST colgroup
    %attrs;
    span            %Number;       "1"
    width           %MultiLength;  #IMPLIED
    %cellhalign;
    %cellvalign;
    >
```

```
<!--
col elements define the alignment properties for cells in
one or more columns.

The width attribute specifies the width of the columns,
e.g.

     width=64         width in screen pixels
     width=0.5*        relative width of 0.5

The span attribute causes the attributes of one
col element to apply to more than one column.
-->
<!ATTLIST col
  %attrs;
  span              %Number;           "1"
  width             %MultiLength;      #IMPLIED
  %cellhalign;
  %cellvalign;
  >

<!--
    Use thead to duplicate headers when breaking table
    across page boundaries, or for static headers when
    tbody sections are rendered in scrolling panel.

    Use tfoot to duplicate footers when breaking table
    across page boundaries, or for static footers when
    tbody sections are rendered in scrolling panel.

    Use multiple tbody sections when rules are needed
    between groups of table rows.
-->
<!ATTLIST thead
  %attrs;
  %cellhalign;
  %cellvalign;
  >

<!ATTLIST tfoot
  %attrs;
  %cellhalign;
  %cellvalign;
  >
```

```
<!ATTLIST tbody
  %attrs;
  %cellhalign;
  %cellvalign;
  >

<!ATTLIST tr
  %attrs;
  %cellhalign;
  %cellvalign;
  >


<!-- Scope is simpler than headers attribute for common
tables -->
<!ENTITY % Scope "(row|col|rowgroup|colgroup)">

<!-- th is for headers, td for data and for cells acting as
both -->

<!ATTLIST th
  %attrs;
  abbr            %Text;          #IMPLIED
  axis            CDATA           #IMPLIED
  headers         IDREFS          #IMPLIED
  scope           %Scope;         #IMPLIED
  rowspan         %Number;        "1"
  colspan         %Number;        "1"
  %cellhalign;
  %cellvalign;
  >

<!ATTLIST td
  %attrs;
  abbr            %Text;          #IMPLIED
  axis            CDATA           #IMPLIED
  headers         IDREFS          #IMPLIED
  scope           %Scope;         #IMPLIED
  rowspan         %Number;        "1"
  colspan         %Number;        "1"
  %cellhalign;
  %cellvalign;
  >
```

APPENDIX B: CASCADING STYLE SHEETS (CSS) FORMATTING PROPERTIES

Font Properties

Property	Description	Value Example(s)
`font`	Global font declaration. Can define all font properties in one property.	`Font-family, font-style, font-weight, font-size, font-style`
`font-family`	Font type to display text	`arial, courier`
`font-size`	Size of font in pixels or as percentage	`small, x-small, medium, large, x-large`
`font-style`	Style of font	`italic, bold, oblique`
`font-varient`	Font rendering	`normal, small-caps`
`font-weight`	Darkness of font. Uses name or number.	`normal, light, bold, bolder, 100, 200, 300, 400,` etc.

Text Properties

Property	Description	Value Example(s)
`word-spacing`	Amount of space between words in an element	`normal`, number of pixels
`letter-spacing`	Amount of space between letters	`normal`, number of pixels
`text-align`	Horizontal alignment of text on page	`right, left, center`
`vertical-align`	Vertical alignment of text on page	`baseline, sub, super, top, text-top, middle, bottom, text-bottom, percentage`
`text-indent`	How much first line is indented	`0`, number of pixels, percentage
`text-transform`	Change case of text	`uppercase, lowercase, capitalize, none`

Property	Description	Value Example(s)
line-height	Amount of space between lines of text	normal, number of pixels
text-decoration	Special controls of text appearance	underline, overline, blink, line-through, none

Color Properties

Property	Description	Value Example(s)
color	Text color	red, blue, color code
background	Global background declaration. Can define all background properties in one property.	background-color, background-image, background-position, background-repeat, background-attachment
background-color	Color of element's background	color name, transparent
background-image	Image to be used as background	URL, name of local file
background-attachment	Scrolling of background image with the element	scroll, fixed
background-position	Position of element's background	top, center, bottom, left, right, percentage, number of pixels
background-repeat	Repeat pattern for background image	repeat, repeat-x, repeat-y, no-repeat

Border Properties

Property	Description	Value Example(s)
border-color	Color of the border of an element	red, blue, color code
border-width	Width of the border	medium, thin, thick, number of pixels

Property	Description	Value Example(s)
border-style	Style of border	none, solid, double
margin-top	Width of margin at the top of element	0, number of pixels, percentage
margin-bottom	Width of margin at the bottom of element	0, number of pixels, percentage
margin-left	Width of margin at the left side of element	0, number of pixels, percentage
margin-right	Width of margin at the right side of element	0, number of pixels, percentage
padding-top	Amount of padding at top of element	0, number of pixels, percentage
padding-bottom	Amount of padding at bottom of element	0, number of pixels, percentage
padding-left	Amount of padding at left side of element	0, number of pixels, percentage
padding-right	Amount of padding at right side of element	0, number of pixels, percentage
clear	Whether an element permits other elements on its sides	none, left, right
float	Floating element	none, left, right
height	Height of an element	auto, number of pixels, percentage
width	Width of section	auto, number of pixels, percentage

Display Properties

Property	Description	Value Example(s)
display	Controls display of element	block, inline, list-item
white-space	Whitespace formatting	normal, pre, nowrap
visibility	Controls visibility of element	inherit, visible, hidden

APPENDIX C: CONVERTING HTML TO XHTML

As you have learned throughout this book, XHTML documents are compatible with older HTML-based browsers. Because most current Web pages are written in HTML, many webmasters will be given the job of converting HTML to XHTML.

HTML to XHTML Conversion Example

Following are the rules you will need to follow in order to convert an HTML document to XHTML.

1. **All markup elements must be lowercase:**

   HTML: `<TITLE>Sample Document</TITLE>`

   XHTML: `<title>Sample Document</title>`

2. **Every open tag must have a corresponding closing tag:**

   HTML:
   ```
   <ol>
          <li>First
          <li>Second
          <li>Third
   </ol>
   ```

   XHTML:
   ```
   <ol>
          <li>First</li>
          <li>Second</li>
          <li>Third</li>
   </ol>
   ```

3. **Empty elements must follow the correct empty-element syntax:**

   HTML: `<BR>`

   XHTML: `<br />`

4. **Every attribute must have a value. The value needs to be surrounded by either single or double quote marks:**

   HTML: `<img src=image1.jpg usemap>`

   XHTML: `<img src="image1.jpg" usemap="usemap" />`

5. **Proper nesting of elements is required:**

   HTML: `<p><em>Proper nesting is required</p></em>`

   XHTML: `<p><em>Proper nesting is required</em></p>`

6. All XHTML documents must contain a DOCTYPE declaration and may, optionally, contain an XML declaration:

```
<?xml version="1.0"?>
<!DOCTYPE html PUBLIC "-//W3C//DTD XHTML 1.0 Strict//EN"
"http://www.w3.org/TR/xhtml1/DTD/xhtml1-strict.dtd">
```

7. The root element `<html>` **must contain an XHTML namespace:**

```
<html xmlns="http://www.w3.org/1999/xhtml">
```

Now, let's take an HTML document and convert it step by step.

```
1  <HTML>
2    <HEAD>
3      <TITLE>Introduction to XHTML</TITLE>
4    </HEAD>
5    <BODY>
6      <STRONG>Course Name:</STRONG> Introduction to XHTML <BR>
7      <STRONG>Course Number:</STRONG> CS 112 <BR>
8      <STRONG>Instructor: </STRONG> Tabitha Perdue <BR>
9      <STRONG>Meeting Time: </STRONG> Wednesday, 5:30pm—7:30pm <BR>
10     <P>
11     <STRONG>Course Description: </STRONG> This course covers the
                basics of how to write XHTML Web documents.
12     <IMG SRC=courseimg.jpg ALT="Introduction to XHTML">
13     <P>
14     <STRONG>Prerequisites: </STRONG>
15     <UL>
16       <LI>CS 101—Introduction to Computers
17       <LI>CS 103—Introduction to Web Site Design
18       <LI>CS 110—Designing Web Pages with HTML
19     </UL>
20   </BODY>
21 </HTML>
```

Step 1: Add the DOCTYPE Declaration and the Optional XML Declaration:

```
1  <?xml version="1.0"?>
2  <!DOCTYPE html PUBLIC "-//W3C//DTD XHTML 1.0 Transitional//EN"
      "http://www.w3.org/TR/xhtml1/DTD/xhtml1-transitional.dtd">
```

Step 2: Add the XHTML Namespace to the Root Element:

```
3  <html xmlns="http://www.w3.org/1999/xhtml">
```

Step 3: Follow the Rules to Create a Well-Formed Document:

a. Change tags to lowercase.

b. Add end tags to all open tags.

c. Create proper syntax for empty elements.

d. Add values and quotes to all attributes.

All changes other than changing all tags to lowercase are below in red.

```
4   <head>
5     <title>Introduction to XHTML</title>
6   </head>
7   <body>
8     <p>
9     <strong>Course Name:</strong>  Introduction to XHTML <br />
10    <strong>Course Number: </strong>  CS 112 <br />
11    <strong>Instructor: </strong> Tabitha Perdue <br />
12    <strong>Meeting Time: </strong> Wednesday, 5:30pm–7:30pm <br />
13    <img src="courseimg.jpg" alt="Introduction to XHTML">
14    </p>
15    <p>
16    <strong>Course Description: </strong> This course covers the
            basics of how to write XHTML Web documents.
17    </p>
18    <strong>Prerequisites: </strong>
19    <ul>
20      <li>CS 101—Introduction to Computers </li>
21      <li>CS 103—Introduction to Web Site Design </li>
22      <li>CS 110—Designing Web Pages with HTML </li>
23    </ul>
24  </body>
25 </html>
```

◎◎ Using Style Sheets to Replace HTML Styles

Many HTML style-related elements have been disapproved of and are excluded from XHTML Strict. These styles can be replaced by using Cascading Style Sheets. Following is an example of an HTML document that uses the `<font>` element to define the style of text:

HTML code:

```
<font color=red face=helvetica>This content is red</font>
```

The <font> element is not included in the DTD for XHTML, so we will assign a class for the <div> element for this style as a replacement:

CSS code:
```
div.red {
             color: red;
             font-family: helvetica
        }
```

XHTML code:
```
<div class="red">This content is red</div>
```

◎◉ Using HTML Tidy to Automate Conversion

The example above walks you through manually converting an HTML document to XHTML. There are tools that can make the job far less tedious. The tool that is supported by the W3C is Tidy, created by Dave Raggett. This application is free and can be downloaded from the Web. Following is the Web address for Tidy, which is included on the W3C Web site:

`http://www.w3.org/People/Raggett/tidy/`

Following are examples of the things Tidy can do for you automatically:

1. Detects and corrects missing or mismatched end tags

2. Corrects end tags that are in the wrong order, to create proper nesting of elements

3. Fixes heading emphasis problems

4. Recovers from mixed-up tags

5. Adds the missing backslash (/) in empty elements

6. Perfects lists by putting in missing tags

7. Adds missing quotes around attribute values

8. Spots tags that are missing a terminating bracket (>)

Tidy can be run from the command line in DOS or Unix, which will allow you to write scripts to further automate the conversion process. Tidy also has a Windows-based GUI version. Figure C.1 is a screenshot from the Tidy GUI application.

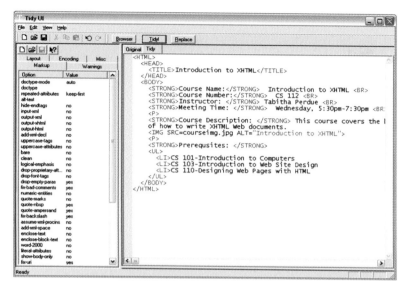

Figure C.1 Tidy GUI Application

Both the command line and GUI versions of this application are easy to use, and well documented on the W3C Web site.

APPENDIX D: ANSWERS TO ODD-NUMBERED HANDS-ON EXERCISES

◎ Chapter 1

1. XHTML 1.0: `http://www.w3.org/TR/xhtml1/`
   XHTML 1.1: `http://www.w3.org/TR/xhtml11/`

3. Screenshot is Figure 1.7

5. Validate page at the following: `http://validator.w3.org/`

◎ Chapter 2

1.
```
<?xml version="1.0"?>
<!DOCTYPE html PUBLIC "-//W3C//DTD XHTML 1.0 Strict//EN"
   "http://www.w3.org/TR/xhtml1/DTD/xhtml1-strict.dtd">
<html xmlns="http://www.w3.org/1999/xhtml">
<head><title>Exercise 1</title></head>
<body>
    <p>
       Popular Pets
       <br />
    </p>
    <ul>
       <li>Dog</li>
       <li>Cat</li>
       <li>Iguana</li>
    </ul>
</body>
</html>
```

3.
```
<?xml version="1.0"?>
<!DOCTYPE html PUBLIC "-//W3C//DTD XHTML 1.0 Strict//EN"
   "http://www.w3.org/TR/xhtml1/DTD/xhtml1-strict.dtd">
<html xmlns="http://www.w3.org/1999/xhtml">
<head>
   <title>XHTML Block-level Elements</title>
</head>
<body>
   <div> This is a paragraph about African Gray parrots.
      The African Gray is one of the most popular pet
      birds of the parrot family. It is known for its
```

```
            intelligence and is one of the best talkers of all
            domesticated birds. This parrot is native to Africa
            and can live to be almost 70 years old.</div>
        <div> This is also a paragraph about African Gray
            parrots. Here is some additional information about
            the African Gray parrot separated by line breaks:
            (break here) <br />The African Gray parrot is about
            15 inches long and (break here) <br />has a wing
            span of about 20 inches.
            <hr />
        </div>
        <div>
            <h1>This is a level 1 heading</h1>
            <h2>This is a level 2 heading</h2>
            <h3>This is a level 3 heading</h3>
            <h4>This is a level 4 heading</h4>
            <h5>This is a level 5 heading</h5>
            <h6>This is a level 6 heading</h6>
            <hr />
        </div>
    </body>
    </html>

5.  <?xml version="1.0"?>
    <!DOCTYPE html PUBLIC "-//W3C//DTD XHTML 1.0 Strict//EN"
       "http://www.w3.org/TR/xhtml1/DTD/xhtml1-strict.dtd">
    <html xmlns="http://www.w3.org/1999/xhtml">
    <head>
        <title>XHTML Lists</title>
    </head>
    <body>
        <p>Weekly Planner</p>
        <ol>
            <li>Monday
                <ul>
                    <li>Pick up dry cleaning</li>
                    <li>Take dog to the vet</li>
                </ul>
            </li>
            <li>Tuesday</li>
            <li>Wednesday
                <ul>
                    <li>Change oil in car</li>
                    <li>Lunch with Wendy</li>
                    <li>Meeting with accountant</li>
                </ul>
            </li>
```

```
        <li>Thursday
           <ul>
              <li>Go to grocery store</li>
              <li>Pay phone bill</li>
           </ul>
        </li>
        <li>Friday
           <ul>
              <li>Dinner and movie</li>
           </ul>
        </li>
        <li>Saturday</li>
        <li>Sunday
           <ul>
              <li>Football game</li>
           </ul>
        </li>
     </ol>
     <p>Robin Williams Movies</p>
     <ul>
        <li>Mrs. Doubtfire</li>
        <li>Peter Pan</li>
        <li>One Hour Photo</li>
     </ul>
  </body>
  </html>
```

◉◉ Chapter 3

1.
```
<link rel="stylesheet" href="
http://www.chughes.com/styles.css" type="text/css" />
```

3.
```
a:link {
      color: green
      }
a:visited {
      color: purple
      }
a:active {
      color: red
      }
a:hover {
      color: blue
      }
```

```
5. h1{
     font-style:bold;
     font-size:22;
     color:green;
     text-align:center;
     display:block;
     padding:25
     }
   p     {
     text-align:left;
     font-size:12;
     color:purple;
     display:block
     }
   h2    {
     text-align:right;
     vertical-aligh:top;
     font-size:12;
     color:red;
     display:block
   }
   div {
     border-style:double;
     width:350;
     padding:15
     }
```

◉◎ Chapter 4

```
1. <img src="sunset.jpg" alt="Picture of a sunset"
   style="border-width:4; padding-top:20; padding-
   bottom:20"   />

3. <?xml version="1.0" ?>
       <!DOCTYPE html PUBLIC "-//W3C//DTD XHTML 1.0
   Strict//EN"
       "http://www.w3.org/TR/xhtml1/DTD/xhtml1-strict.dtd">
   <html xmlns="http://www.w3.org/1999/xhtml">
   <head>
      <title>WAV File</title>
   </head>
   <body>
      <div>
          Click on the link below to play the bell
          <br />
```

```
        <a href="bell.wav">Bell .wav file</a>
        <br />
    </div>
</body>
</html>
```

5.
```
<?xml version="1.0" ?>
    <!DOCTYPE html PUBLIC "-//W3C//DTD XHTML 1.0 Strict//EN"
    "http://www.w3.org/TR/xhtml1/DTD/xhtml1-strict.dtd">
<html xmlns="http://www.w3.org/1999/xhtml">
<head>
    <title>WAV File</title>
    <style type="text/css">
    <!--
    object {
        border-stle: thin;
        margin-left: 50%
        }
    -->
    </style>
</head>
<body>
    <p>
        <object classid="clsid:8E27C92B-1264-101C-
            8A2F-040224009C02">
        <param name="BackColor" value="14544622" />
        <param name="DayLength" value="1" />
        </object>
    </p>
</body>
</html>
```

◎◎ Chapter 5

1.
```
<?xml version="1.0" encoding="utf-8"?>
    <!DOCTYPE html PUBLIC "-//W3C//DTD XHTML 1.0
Strict//EN"
    "http://www.w3.org/TR/xhtml1/DTD/xhtml1-strict.dtd">
<html xmlns="http://www.w3.org/1999/xhtml">
<head>
    <title>Table Example in XHTML</title>
</head>
```

```
<body>
    <div style="align:center"><h1>Our First
        Table</h1></div>
    <!--  Begin Table -->
    <table frame="box" rules="rows">
        <caption>A Simple Table of Columns and Rows
        </caption>
        <!--  Begin First Row -->
        <tr>
            <th>Column 1</th>
            <th>Column 2</th>
            <th>Column 3</th>
        </tr>
        <!--  End First Row -->
        <!--  Begin Second Row -->
        <tr>
            <td>Column 1 <br /> Row 2</td>
            <td>Column 2 <br /> Row 2</td>
            <td>Column 3 <br /> Row 2</td>
        </tr>
        <!--  End Second Row -->
        <!--  Begin Third Row -->
        <tr>
            <td>Column 1 <br /> Row 3</td>
            <td>Column 2 <br /> Row 3</td>
            <td>Column 3 <br /> Row 3</td>
        </tr>
            <!--  End Third Row -->
    </table>
    <!--  End Table -->
</body>
</html>

3. <?xml version="1.0" encoding="utf-8"?>
    <!DOCTYPE html PUBLIC "-//W3C//DTD XHTML 1.0
Strict//EN"
    "http://www.w3.org/TR/xhtml1/DTD/xhtml1-strict.dtd">
<html xmlns="http://www.w3.org/1999/xhtml">
<head>
    <title>Spanning Multiple Table Rows and Columns
        With XHTML Tables</title>
    <style type="text/css">
        .outer {
            background-color: "#993366"
            }
```

```
    .inner {
       background-color: "#666666";
       color: white
       }
    caption {color: black}
  </style>
</head>
<body>
  <!--  Begin Outer Table -->
  <table border="1" cellpadding="15" class="inner">
     <caption><strong>Daycare Child ID Card
     </strong></caption>
     <!-- Begin First Row -->
     <tr class="outer">
        <th><big>Photo:</big></th>
        <th class="outer" colspan="2">
           <big>Identification Card</big></td>
     </tr>
     <tr>
        <td rowspan="7" class="outer">
           <img src="kylie.jpg"></td>
     </tr>
     <tr>
        <td><strong>Name:</strong></td>
        <td>Kylie Fraser</td>
     </tr>
     <tr>
        <td><strong>Address:</strong></td>
        <td>9 Perdue Ln.<br>Boston, MA 02109</td>
     </tr>
     <tr>
        <td><strong>Parents:</strong></td>
        <td>Mother: Julie Fraser<br>Father: Brad
           Fraser</td>
     </tr>
     <tr>
        <td><strong>Contact Numbers:</strong>
           </td>
        <td>Home: 617-555-1212<br>
           Mobile: 617-123-1234<br>
           Work: 617-444-6666</td>
     </tr>
     <tr>
        <td><strong>Medical Information:
           </strong></td>
```

```
         <td>Blood Type: O<br>Allergies: Peanuts
            <br>Medications: none</td>
      </tr>
      <tr>
         <td><strong>Other Information:</strong>
            </td><td>None</td>
      </tr>
   </table>
</body>
</html>
```

5. Use the site at `http://validator.w3.org/`

◎◎ Chapter 6

1. ```
<!DOCTYPE html
    PUBLIC "-//W3C//DTD XHTML 1.0 Frameset//EN"
    "http://www.w3.org/TR/xhtml1/DTD/xhtml1-frameset.dtd">
<html xmlns="http://www.w3.org/1999/xhtml">
<head>
    <title>Our First Frame Document</title>
</head>
<frameset cols="33%,33%,33%">
    <frame src="frame1.html" />
    <frame src="frame2.html" />
    <frame src="frame3.html" />
</frameset>
</html>
```

3. ```
<?xml version="1.0"?>
   <!DOCTYPE html PUBLIC "-//W3C//DTD XHTML 1.0
Frameset//EN"
    "http://www.w3.org/TR/xhtml1/DTD/xhtml1-frameset.dtd">
    <html xmlns="http://www.w3.org/1999/xhtml">
<head>
    <title>Our First Frame Document</title>
</head>
<frameset cols="25%,50%,25%">
    <frame src="frame1.html" />
<frameset rows="100%">
    <frame src="nested-frame1.html" />
</frameset>
    <frame src="frame2.html" />
</frameset>
```

5. Site: `http://www.w3.org/TR/xframes/`

XFrames addresses the issues with:

☆ usability

☆ searching of frame documents

☆ security

◎◉ Chapter 7

```
1. <?xml version="1.0"?>
      <!DOCTYPE html PUBLIC "-//W3C//DTD XHTML 1.0     |
         Transitional//EN"
      "http://www.w3.org/TR/xhtml1/DTD/
         xhtml1-transitional.dtd">
   <html xmlns="http://www.w3.org/1999/xhtml">
   <head>
      <title>Login Page</title>
      <link rel="stylesheet" href="exercise-4.css"
         type="text/css" />
   </head>
   <body>
      <center>
      <div class="card">
         <h1>Please Log In</h1>
      <div class="login">
      <form>
         <p>
            Name: <input type="text" size="30">
         </p>
         <p>
            Password: <input type="text" size="30">
         </p>
         <p>
            <input type="submit" value="Login">  
            <input type="reset" value="reset">
         </p>
      </form>
      </div>
      </div>
      </center>
   </body>
   </html>
```

3. ```
   <input type="checkbox" name="Classes" value="1101" />
       Introduction to Shakespeare <br />
   <input type="checkbox" name="Classes" value="2119"  />
       Advanced Computer Networking <br />
   <input type="checkbox" name="Classes" value="5428"  />
       History of Philosophy <br />
   <input type="checkbox" name="Classes" value="8759"  />
       Statistical Analysis <br />
   ```

5. Cascading Style Sheet (CSS):
   ```
   h1 {
       font-style:bold;
       font-size:22;
       color:purple;
       text-align:center;
       display:block;
       padding:10
       }
   div.login {
       text-align:left;
       font-size:12;
       font-color:red;
       display:block
       }
   .block {
       display:block
       }
   .phone {
       text-align:right;
       vertical-aligh:top;
       font-size:12;
       font-color:black;
       display:block
       }
   .card {
       border-style:solid;
       width:350;
       top-margin:30pt;
       align:center;
       padding:15
       }
   ```
   ```

◎◎ Chapter 8

1. `<!DOCTYPE html PUBLIC "-//W3C//DTD XHTML 2.0//EN" "TBD">`

3. XHTML 1.0—Meant to be a transition from HTML to XHTML. Contains most of the element set of HTML 4.0.1.

   XHTML 1.1—Created a module-based XHTML language. This version does not support many of the presentational elements in HTML.

   XHTML 2.0—Like XHTML 1.1, XHTML 2.0 is modular in form. This version is not meant to be compatible with older versions.

   XHTML Basic—Core set of XHTML element set meant for use with small client devices such as cell phones and PDAs.

5. The XForms module is a part of the Modularization of XHTML. As an independent module, it can be used in conjunction with the XHTML base language and other modules in order to create XHTML forms.

INDEX

Web-Safe Colors

Most computers can display millions of colors, but they do not display all colors consistently. For example, one computer may display a Web page with a dark red background, whereas another displays the same Web page with a brown background. To ensure that your Web pages look the same to everyone, select your colors from the following palette of 216 Web-safe colors. These colors will always look the same (or at least very close to the same) on all computer platforms and computer monitors.